# THE
# ANCIENT
# WAY

## TAMARA LANCASTIE

My 4-year journey 2014-2018, and so it continues…

A catalogue record for this book is available from the National Library of New Zealand

Front Cover Base Image: Johannes Plenio (Unsplash.com)
Cover Design: Colleen Kaluza
All internal images are used with permission

Edited and Published by WordWyze
Printed by YourBooks.com
Published & Printed in New Zealand

Softcover ISBN: 978-0-473-48001-1
Epub ISBN: 978-0-473-48002-8

# CONTENTS

# ACKNOWLEDGEMENTS

First and foremost, all acknowledgement,
thanks and praise goes to Yahweh
for pushing me to write this all down
(hopefully He is proud of my attempt).

Secondly, to my dear friend, Ana,
who was brave enough to read my draft
all the way through, thank you
for all your encouragement!

And thirdly, to Colleen, my editor,
for all her encouragement too.

What a blessing you all are!

# FOREWORD

The following are my thoughts on how I see my walk with the Lord. I share this not to argue; my sincere hope is that, though you may not agree with me, you will endeavour to try and understand where I am coming from. Let me make it abundantly clear from the outset: I am not becoming a Jew, I am not taking on the "Jewish" feasts, I am not taking on the Talmud (the oral law); these are what Yeshua (Jesus) taught against - the doctrines and traditions of men. I do plan on discussing here, the upholding of the law, the Sabbath rest, Yahweh's/God's appointed feast days, unclean food, Christmas and Easter.

My prayer is that you will read this with an open mind.

**NOTE**: Throughout this book, any emphasis added to Scriptures quoted (underlines, all caps or bold), are mine.

So, here are some questions to think about regarding God's Law[1]:

1) If we have been freed from the Law of God (the Torah), and the Law of God is freedom (Psalms 119:44-45), is that saying that we can be freed from freedom?

2) If the law of God has been made better, and the law of God is perfect, is that saying that what is already defined as perfect, can be made better?

3) Can Truth be made not Truth? (Psalms 119:143, 160)

4) Can what defines sin be nullified? Can sin be sin one day and not sin another day? Does the definition of sin change?

5) If God is the Word, and God cannot change, then how can we suggest that the Word of God changed? (John 1:1, Malachi 3:6, Hebrews 1:12 and 13:8)

6) If Christ is the Word made flesh (John 1:14), and Christ is the Word of God (John 1; Revelation 19:13), and supposedly some of the

---

[1] Questions adapted from 119 Ministries, *The Unanswerable Questions*. (n.d.). Retrieved from https://www.119ministries.com/teachings/video-teachings/detail/the-unanswerable-questions/ *Used with permission.*

Word of God is abolished, did He get on the cross to abolish parts of Himself?

7) If the Law of God is all about loving God and loving others: is how to love God and how to love others subject to change?
(Matthew 22:35-37)

8) If the Law of God is forever, and the law of God ended, as some believe, is that saying that forever can end?  Does that mean eternal life can end as well?

9) If we are to delight in the Law of God (the Torah) (Psalms 1:2;  Psalms 110; Romans 7:22) are we to no longer delight in it?

10) In Isaiah 66:15-17, we see that in the context of the Lord's return He is clearly upset that people are eating pork.  If He cares enough to establish the law in Leviticus and Deuteronomy and cares later in Isaiah, why would we assume that He doesn't care now?

11) When Yeshua commanded us to observe and do everything said from Moses' seat (Matthew 23:1-3), which is the Law of Yahweh written by Moses, then why would we not want to do it? Since Yeshua commands us to teach all nations everything He commanded, surely this would include everything taught from the seat of Moses?

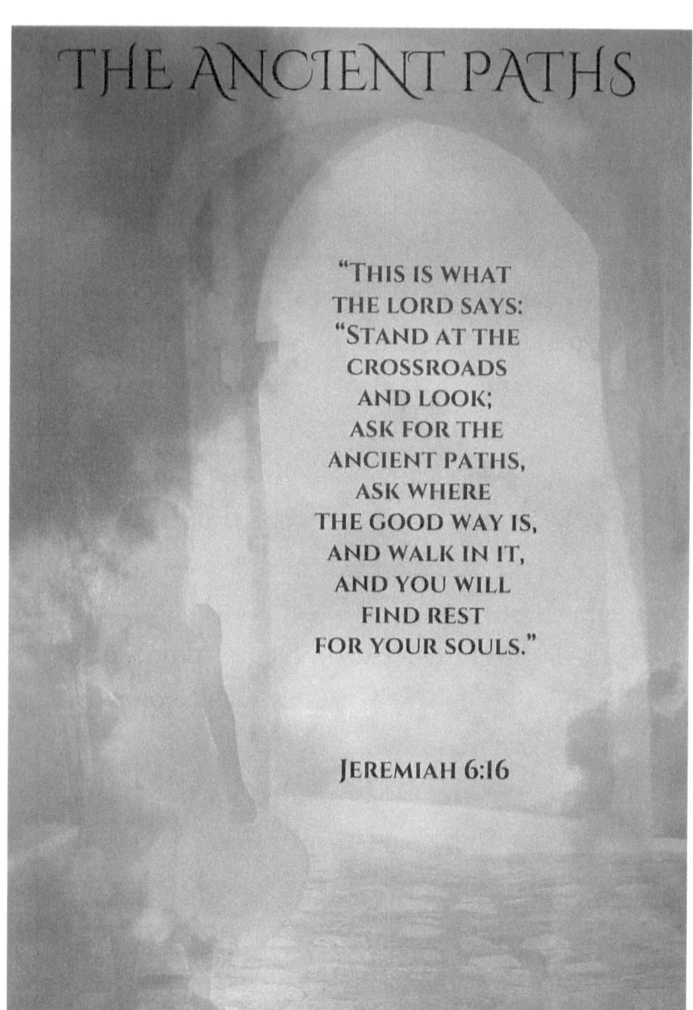
THE ANCIENT PATHS

"THIS IS WHAT
THE LORD SAYS:
"STAND AT THE
CROSSROADS
AND LOOK;
ASK FOR THE
ANCIENT PATHS,
ASK WHERE
THE GOOD WAY IS,
AND WALK IN IT,
AND YOU WILL
FIND REST
FOR YOUR SOULS."

JEREMIAH 6:16

# 1

# UPHOLDING THE LAW AND NOT FOLLOWING TRADITION

Many say that it is impossible to keep the law, but the Bible says that there are those who did keep all the laws, like Zechariah and Elizabeth in Luke 1:6, the apostle Paul and, of course, Yeshua. Perhaps it is a matter of choice and desire, and not as complicated as we think? Let us take a look at what the Bible says. Yeshua himself is saying in Matthew 5:17-19:

> "Do not think that I have come to abolish the law or the Prophets, think not that I have come to abolish them but to fulfil[2] them. I tell you the truth, until heaven and earth disappear not the

---

2     Strong's reference G4137 for "Fulfil" does not mean "to do away with". "Fulfil"  Meaning: to render perfect, carry out, to supply, verify.

*smallest letter, not the least stroke of the pen, will by any means disappear from the Law until everything is accomplished. Anyone who breaks one of the least of these commandments and teaches others to do the same, they will be called least in the kingdom of heaven, but whoever practices and teaches these commands will be called great in the kingdom of heaven."*

Have heaven and earth disappeared yet? No. Have a re-read of these verses - what else does it say? We know that heaven and earth have not disappeared as we can confirm to this day; therefore, the law still exists. You will see that the verse goes on to say, that "If anyone breaks the least of these commandments…" This clearly suggests that the commandments are still in play. What these verses do not say is that if you do not keep the law and commandments, you will not make it into the kingdom of heaven. This should be a huge relief, but you will be considered the least and will not be so esteemed as your fellow brothers and sisters who kept the commandments. Nonetheless, the recognition of this fact should not stop us from endeavouring to follow His commands (Philippians 3:14 and Colossians 1:29).

Even Paul, in Romans 3:31, says that we must uphold the law; faith does not nullify the law.

Romans 6:15-23 says we are not to sin, that is, break the law, we are now slaves to righteousness. Neither Paul nor we can break the Sabbath and still "uphold the law".

Romans 2:13

> *"For not the hearers of the law are just before God, but the doers of the law shall be justified."*

Paul also adds in Romans 7:12

> *"The law is holy, and the commandment holy, and just, and good."*

So, Paul could not have said it is good and have kept the laws, but at the same time say it doesn't matter anymore, as suggested in other Scriptures written by Paul. This would be a contradiction and the Bible, as the infallible word of God, cannot contradict itself. Perhaps the teachings of Paul have been misunderstood?

We have been warned in Scripture by Peter (2 Peter 3:16), that Paul's writings are hard to understand, and are distorted by other people, including other Scriptures.

If Paul's writings were difficult to understand at that time, with the cultural knowledge and comprehension of the actual wording of that day, then how can we expect to understand any better now, with the translational issues, the lack of cultural awareness and the distance of time, 2000 years later? Just on the law of keeping the Sabbath day holy alone, there are over 100 verses in the Bible that refer to this, including verses found in the New Testament.

This law of keeping the Sabbath is discussed further in the "Shabbat (Sabbath Day)" chapter.

There is a danger of people taking things too far, by bringing in doctrines and traditions of men (the oral law) that are unnecessary. It is entirely reasonable to suggest that in our modern, enlightened times, Christians do this too, and not just the Pharisees in the Bible. Think Anglican, Catholicism, how we baptise/dedicate people, Easter eggs and the Easter bunny, the role of women in the church, how/when we take communion? Perhaps our views on the gifts of the Holy Spirit? For example, some Christians and churches believe that the gifts of the Holy Spirit are not for now and it is a thing of the past.

What do we do in our Sunday church or gatherings that may be a tradition or a doctrine? Have you ever asked yourself why we do the things we do?

Mark 7:1-9

> *Then the Pharisees and some of the scribes who had come from Jerusalem gathered around Jesus, and they saw some of His disciples eating with hands that were defiled—that is, unwashed. (Now in <u>holding to the tradition of the elders,</u> the*

*Pharisees and all the Jews do not eat until they wash their hands ceremonially. And on returning from the market, they do not eat unless they wash. And there are many other traditions for them to observe, including the washing of cups, pitchers, kettles, and couches for dining.)*

*So, the Pharisees and scribes questioned Jesus: "Why do Your disciples not walk according to the tradition of the elders? Instead, they eat with defiled hands."*

*Jesus answered them, "Isaiah prophesied correctly about you hypocrites, as it is written:*

*THESE PEOPLE HONOR ME WITH THEIR LIPS, BUT THEIR HEARTS ARE FAR FROM ME. THEY WORSHIP ME IN VAIN; THEY TEACH AS DOCTRINE THE PRECEPTS OF MEN.'*

*You have disregarded the commandment of God to keep the tradition of men." He went on to say, "<u>You neatly set aside the commandment of God to maintain your own tradition.</u>"*

It was the way in which they washed their hands, that was the issue; the disciples did not follow the "correct" way of doing things. The Pharisees added extra traditions and doctrines (Oral Law) to the Scriptures.

Peter's vision in Acts 10, portraying unclean animals, is another example of a cultural issue that even the apostles needed to rectify. Peter said to Yahweh that he would never eat anything unclean. He backed this up with Scripture to the Lord, but there was never anything in the law, within the Scriptures, to corroborate not associating with gentiles. Yahweh used this vision to test Peter, and Peter passed this test with flying colours. Peter himself makes it clear that the interpretation is about not calling gentiles unclean. So, where do we get, from Peter's own interpretation, that unclean foods have now become clean, as commonly preached in the modern church?

Acts 10:28

> *"He said to them, "You know how unlawful it is for a Jew to associate with a foreigner or visit him. But God has shown me that I should not call any man impure or unclean."*

In Peter's day, the Jews did not associate with Gentiles, even the "Messianic" Jews, the Yeshua-believing Israelites, struggled with the traditions from their oral law of not associating with the Gentiles, hence this vision from the Lord to Peter. As a result of the vision, Peter invites the three men to stay overnight, before setting off to stay with the Captain. This would have been totally unacceptable for Jews at this time. This vision had to happen; otherwise, Peter would never have gone to Cornelius, and all that transpired would not have taken place. The Holy Spirit would not have come upon the believing "Gentiles", and the believing Jews would not have realised that "Elohim has indeed given to the nations, repentance to life", Acts 1:18. The Holy Spirit was already familiar to the Israelites, just not so to the Gentiles.

The Pharisees also tried to bring Yeshua into blaspheming against Yahweh, with a discussion on what is lawful on the Sabbath. Yeshua says that it is good to help an animal in distress on the Sabbath and to heal those who need healing, to save a life (Mark 3:1-5). These are good things and bring glory to Yahweh. Yeshua would have been arrested then and there if he had broken the commandments and the laws of God of not working on the Sabbath. The Pharisees were just waiting for any excuse, but not once did Yeshua transgress the law.

1 Peter 2:22

> *"He committed no sin, and no deceit was found in his mouth."*

One needs to remember that there was no New Testament at this time, the only Scriptures were the Tanakh (now commonly known as the Old Testament). Three-quarters of the Bible is the Old Testament. Many Christians dismiss the commandments and the moedim, the Lord's appointed times and festivals (if they are even aware of them), and say it is Old Testament and "done away with", and therefore not relevant anymore. But these same people, and I have been guilty of that, love reading Psalms and Proverbs and applying the wisdom of some of these verses to their lives. I call it cherry picking.

Proverbs and Psalms were also written by the Israelites, and much of these chapters refer to the Torah, the law (instructions). If we say that the Old Testament is done away with, should not Christians disregard Psalms and Proverbs as well? Why are these two books any different? How do we so easily decide what is relevant or not?

King David wrote many Psalms, and we know that he was described as a man after God's own heart, who will do "all My will", that is God's will, as shown in Acts 13:22. Throughout his writings, he constantly talks about Yahweh's "right-rulings", "your Torah I have not forgotten", "I have loved your Torah", "I observe the commands of my God", "always look to Your laws", "I have loved your commands", "all your orders I count as right", "all Your commands are truth", "all your commands are righteous". I think you get the picture? So much importance has been placed on David throughout the Bible, and we know our Messiah comes from the line of David.

We cannot dismiss the Old Testament as irrelevant and only for the Jews, as the New Testament hinges on the Old. This death of the Messiah is prophesied in the Old Testament; everything in the "new" is backed up by the Old Testament, as seen with some examples below, regarding Yeshua's death.

John 19:24 cross-reference with Psalms 22:18;

John 19:36 cross-reference with Exodus 12:46, Numbers 9:12 and Psalms 34:20;

John 19:37 cross-reference with Zechariah 12:10.

Without the Old Testament, there could be no New Testament and therefore no Yeshua the Messiah. Getting rid of the old would make no sense of the new, as the New Testament is a continuation of the old, and is totally built on the Old Testament, the Tanakh. Yeshua (meaning Salvation) will restore all things (Acts 3:20-21). God made all things good and never intended things to change. If man had not sinned, all would still be perfect.

Yeshua was a Jew, he ate like a Jew, lived like a Jew, from the royal line of David, was circumcised and was perfect in every way, obeying all the laws and commandments, unblemished, the holy son of Yahweh. He came to this earth and allowed himself to suffer and to be sacrificed (our Passover lamb) so that we could be set free from the *punishment*, the curse, of our sins, to be our mediator, so that we can be in closer relationship with the one true God, Yahweh. His blood and death were the atonement for our sins, and his spilt blood has redeemed us. It is Yeshua's spilt blood, his horrendous, tortuous, tragic death that has set us free from all guilt (no condemnation), so that we may be saved and have eternal life and come freely to our heavenly father, Yahweh.

1 John 2:2-4

> *"He Himself is the atoning sacrifice for our sins, and not for ours alone, but also for the sins of the whole world. By this, we can be sure that we have come to know Him: if we keep His commandments. If anyone says, "I know Him," but does not keep His commandments, he is a liar, and the truth is not in him..."*

The last sentence of the above verse has uncomfortably strong words. Keeping His commands is written in black and white.

Many say that Yeshua did away with the Law at his death and resurrection and that we are now under a new covenant, but how can this be? A new covenant doesn't mean a new law.

For example, if one decides to live in a rental property which has a body corporate, then the tenant agrees to abide by the rules of the body corporate and signs the agreement/covenant. Should this tenant then decide to move out, and a new tenant comes along, this new tenant agrees to the body corporate rules. The body corporate rules do not change, even though there is a new tenant and a **new covenant** agreement has been signed. The body corporate rules do not become nullified.

The Scriptures say that the law will be written on our hearts, thus suggesting that we will no longer have to teach each other the law and the words of God. We will want to obey his laws and commands.

Ezekiel 36:27

> *"And I will put my Spirit in you and move you to follow my decrees and be careful to keep my laws."*

Jeremiah 31:33-37

> *"This is the covenant I will make with the house of Israel after those days, declares the LORD.*
>
> *I will put My law in their minds and inscribe it on their hearts. And I will be their God, and they will be My people.*
>
> *No longer will each man teach his neighbour or his brother, saying, 'Know the LORD,' because they will all know Me, from the least of them to the greatest, declares the LORD.*
>
> *For I will forgive their iniquities and will remember their sins no more."*
>
> *Thus says the LORD, who gives the sun for light by day and orders the moon and stars for light by night, who stirs up the sea so that its waves roar—the LORD of Hosts is His name:*

*"Only if this fixed order departed from My presence, declares the LORD, would Israel's descendants ever cease to be a nation before Me."*

Although the Scriptures above are referring specifically to the tribes of Israel, we know that along with the tribes that came out of Egypt, whom Yahweh miraculously set free from slavery, there also came a great multitude, non-Israelites. These Gentiles came to keep the commandments and were explicitly mentioned in Exodus and Deuteronomy.

Other Scriptures talk about the olive tree, the natural branches (Israel), and the wild branches (people who are not of the tribes of Israel, but who accept Yeshua and the God of Abraham, Isaac and Jacob) that have been grafted in, to become one tree, feeding off the same root. Therefore, we can have confidence that we are part of Israel. What a blessing! Isn't it also incredible that Yahweh keeps His promises to His people, which is highlighted in the above Scripture, in Jeremiah 31:35 and 36, that Israel will not cease as a nation unless these ordinances cease.

At this stage, we are still teaching each other about the Lord, so clearly, although this "new" covenant has started, it has not been completed. We have already seen in 1 John 2:2-4 that we are called to keep his commandments.  Remember Matthew 5:17-19, at the start of this chapter "...until heaven and earth disappear..."? It is not just to the Jew to keep the commands.  To continue to say that the laws and commandments have been thrown out and are not relevant anymore with the death of Yeshua, would suggest there to be a contradiction in the Bible, and the Bible, Yahweh's living breathing Word, cannot contradict itself.  The Bible is the infallible Word of God, so something doesn't quite add up.   Note that the following Scriptures are found in the "New" Testament.

Hebrews 13:8

> *"Yeshua the Messiah (Jesus Christ) is the same yesterday, today and forever."*

John 14:15

> *"If you love Me, you will keep My commands."*

John 14:21

> *"Whoever has My commandments and keeps them is the one who loves Me. The one who loves Me will be loved by My Father, and I will love him and reveal Myself to him."*

Yeshua re-emphasises keeping Yahweh's (His father) commands, further along in verses 23 and 24 of John 14 below.

> *"He who does not love Me does not keep My words, and the word which you hear is not Mine, but the Fathers who sent Me."*

In John 17:6 and 7, Yeshua, in a prayer to his father, Yahweh, says:

> *"I have revealed Your name to those You have given Me out of the world. They were Yours; You gave them to Me, and they have kept Your word. Now they know that everything You have given to Me comes from You."*

There is much talk of love in these verses. The commandments can be summed up as loving God and loving one another. It is a <u>summary</u>. This does not mean to say that the commandments have been done away with. Remember, Yeshua kept <u>all</u> the commandments and we are to be like Him.

**The law has not been abolished** and nailed to the cross, it is the enmity and dogma that has been abolished and nailed to the cross, i.e. the commands and teachings of men.

Ephesians 2:15-16

> *"Having abolished in His flesh the enmity – the Torah of the commands in dogma – so as to create in Himself one renewed man from the two, thus making peace, and to completely restore favour both of them unto Elohim in one body through the stake, having destroyed the enmity by it."*

You may think that these two verses back up the law having been done away with, but if we go to Colossians 2:14 and 20-22, these verses are more specific and tell us otherwise:

> *"having blotted out that which was written by hand against us – by the dogmas – which stood against us. And He has taken it out of the way, having nailed it to the stake...*

> *If, then, you died with Messiah from the elementary matters of the world, why, as though living in the world, do you subject yourselves to dogmas: "Do not touch, do not taste, do not handle" – which are all to perish with use – according to the <u>commands and teachings of men?</u>"*

This is not referring to Yahweh's laws which He wrote; the above verse is clearly referring to man's laws - quite the difference.

Yes, absolutely, we are "saved" by grace because of Abba Father's mercy.  With this there is no doubt, we cannot be saved by keeping the law, but we show our love for the Lord by obedience to Yahweh, and this includes keeping His ways, His law.

Remember too, that the 10 commandments were written by the hand of God himself, not by Moses, not by man. How special is that?  Yahweh was so serious about his commands that He wrote them himself, and said that they are to be kept forever.

Yeshua is the Word made flesh.

John 1:1-2

> *"In the beginning was the Word, and the Word was with God, and the Word was God.  He was with God in the beginning."*

John 1:14

> *"The Word became flesh and made his dwelling among us. We have seen his glory, the glory of the one and only Son, who came from the Father, full of grace and truth."*

Only the Tanakh (Old Testament) was available at the time of Yeshua, so what is the "Word"?  We are told repeatedly in the "old", that the Way, the

Truth, the Life is Torah. These words are also repeated in the New Testament.

John 14:6

> *"I am the Way, the Truth and the Life. No man comes to the Father except through me."*

So, who is speaking these words and what do they mean? Yeshua is talking, and it means that Yeshua is declaring that He is the Law (the Living Torah); that He is the Word made flesh; that He is the Way; He is Truth, and He is Life; that the Law are these and that He was there at the beginning. This is corroborated with Scripture like the ones shown below.

Psalms 119:1

> *"Blessed are the undefiled in the **WAY**, who walk in the LAW of the LORD."*

Psalms 119:142

> *"Thy righteousness is an everlasting righteousness, and thy LAW is the **TRUTH**."*

Proverbs 13:14

> *"The LAW of the wise is a fountain of **LIFE**, to depart from the snares of death."*

Over and over again, in the Scriptures, we see what is called the Way, the Truth, the Life and even the Light; it is his Torah, God's law, His instructions to those who would be his people.

Some say that we are not Jewish; therefore, we do not have to keep the law, but as already mentioned, we see that the olive tree is used in Scripture to compare us to Israel. If we are indeed grafted in, as Paul says in Romans 11, then are we not Israel? Being Israel, God gives us His commandments, He says that His instructions are to be kept forever, throughout all generations. To be clear, you cannot be saved by keeping the law. **The law/instructions come after salvation**. It is our instruction for righteousness, for right living. They are like a guardrail to protect us.

Proverbs 6:23

> *"For the commandment is a lamp; and the law is light; and reproofs of instruction are the way of life."*

We are still called to obey Him and to sin no more, so what is the definition of sin?

The answer is in 1 John 3:4,

> *"Everyone who sins breaks the law; in fact, sin is lawlessness."*

Verse 6 goes on to say:

> *"No one who lives in him keeps on sinning. No one who continues to sin has either seen him or known him."*

These are strong words, could our Heavenly Father actually feel strongly about this subject?

According to 1 John 3:4, we have found a definition of sin in the Scriptures which mentions law; therefore, there must actually be a law in place; otherwise, there could be no possibility to ever sin and therefore, no possibility of ever breaking the law. It is made clear that there is still sin in this world and in individuals. Considering that the New Testament was not even written/compiled when these words were spoken, then there can only be one set of laws that this is referring to. I put it to you that the law here, is what we know as the 10 commandments as written in Deuteronomy 5:7-21:

> *"I am the LORD your God, who brought you out of Egypt, out of the land of slavery.*

*7 "You shall have no other gods before me.*

*8 "You shall not make for yourself an image in the form of anything in heaven above or on the earth beneath or in the waters below. 9 You shall not bow down to them or worship them; for I, the LORD your God, am a jealous God, punishing the children for the sin of the parents to the third and fourth generation of those who hate me, 10 but showing love to a thousand generations of those who love me and keep my commandments.*

*11 "You shall not misuse the name of the LORD your God, for the LORD will not hold anyone guiltless who misuses his name.*

*12 "Observe the Sabbath day by keeping it holy, as the LORD your God has commanded you. 13 Six days you shall labour and do all your work, 14 but the seventh day is a sabbath to the LORD your God. On it, you shall not do any work, neither you, nor your son or daughter, nor your male or female servant, nor your ox, your donkey or any of your animals, nor any foreigner residing in your towns, so that your male and female servants may rest, as you do. 15 Remember that you were slaves in Egypt and that the LORD your God brought you out of there with a mighty hand and an outstretched arm. Therefore, the LORD your God has commanded you to observe the Sabbath day.*

*16 "Honour your father and your mother, as the LORD your God has commanded you, so that you may live long and that it may go well with you in the land the LORD your God is giving you.*

*17 "You shall not murder.*

*18 "You shall not commit adultery.*

*19 "You shall not steal.*

*20 "You shall not give false testimony against your neighbour.*

*21 "You shall not covet your neighbour's wife. You shall not set your desire on your neighbour's house or land, his male or female servant, his ox or donkey, or anything that belongs to your neighbour."*

*22 These are the commandments the LORD proclaimed in a loud voice to your whole assembly there on the mountain from out of the fire, the cloud and the deep darkness; and he added nothing more. Then he wrote them on two stone tablets and gave them to me.*

Note that the second commandment of having no idol, and the fourth commandment of observing the Sabbath, are the only commandments that Yahweh is long in explanation.

We are also told to pursue perfection in Matthew 5:48: *"be perfect, as your heavenly Father is perfect,"* which we can only hope to obtain by perseverance and through Yahweh's grace, as He continues to refine us as we seek him and pray and humble ourselves and turn from our wicked ways (2 Chronicles 7:14).

If our Heavenly Father is perfect, then how could He have apparently got it so wrong all those years ago, when writing the laws and knowing that His people would stuff it up? He is the author (Hebrews 12:2), He knows everything before we were even born.

2 Corinthians 7:1

> *"Therefore, since we have these promises, dear friends, let us purify ourselves from everything that contaminates body and spirit, perfecting holiness out of reverence for God."*

This Scripture tells us to be holy, in fact, it tells us to perfect holiness in our lives because of our reverence for God. If we love Him, we will want to do this, so how do we become holy? By not sinning, by not breaking the law and by keeping His commands, by being set-apart. This has to include repentance, knowing that our heavenly Father will and does forgive us, and by loving one another.

Remember that there is no condemnation in Yeshua. Guilt comes from Satan, but the Holy Spirit will prick our conscience if we haven't closed our hearts and mind to Him.

We are called to obey the Lord God of heaven and earth, Yahweh the King of kings; to walk in His ways, to walk in His will, to follow Him. We are told in the Scriptures to keep His commands, to be holy, set apart for the Lord, and this includes keeping Sabbath and the Lord's appointed holy days.

1 Peter 2:21

> *"The Messiah also suffered for you and left an example for you to follow in his steps."*

Malachi 3:6

> *"I the LORD do not change…"*

Ephesians 5:1

> *"Be imitators of God…"*

or in the NIV

> *"Follow God's example…"*

Following the ways of the Lord are not plain sailing, and although Scripture does speak of a yoke and a burden, we are told that it will <u>not</u> be difficult to keep His ways, and there is the promise that we will find rest.

Deuteronomy 30:11

> *"Now what I am commanding you today is not too difficult for you or beyond your reach."*

Matthew 11:28-30

> *"Come to Me, all who are weary and heavy-laden, and I will give you rest. "Take My yoke upon you and learn from Me, for I am gentle and humble in heart, and <u>you will find rest for your souls</u>. "For My yoke is easy and My burden is light."*

This same verse in Matthew parallels with Jeremiah 6:16

> *"Thus says Yahweh, "Stand at the crossroads and look; and ask after the <u>ancient paths</u>, where the good way is, and walk in it. <u>And you will find rest for your souls</u>. But they said we will not walk in it..."*

Could it also be, that the modern church is saying that they will not walk in it? What is the ancient path that is 'the good way'? I put it to you that keeping His commands and keeping the moedim (the Lord's appointed times/festivals), is the ancient path, the good way.

Psalms 19:8

> *"The commandments of the LORD are right, bringing joy to the heart. The commands of the LORD are pure, giving insight for living."*

Psalms 12:6

> *"The words of the LORD are flawless, like silver refined in a furnace, like gold purified sevenfold."*

If the words of the Lord (Scripture) are pure or flawless, then we cannot continue to write off huge chunks of Scripture.

2 Timothy 3:16

> *"All Scripture is God-breathed and profitable for teaching, for rebuking, for correcting, and training in righteousness".*

Psalms 40:8

> *"I delight to do Your will, O my God; Your Law is within my heart."*

The law written upon our hearts was not just for the New Testament church after Yeshua was killed. Clearly, it was also back in the "old days", the ancient days, since this was written a long time before He was crucified. The writer of this Psalm knew the law, because it would have been taught to him and practised from birth. It's not too late for us to start to learn now.

We still need to stop sinning, and when we sin, we need to repent. We cannot keep on doing what we've always done if this is contrary to His ways, His laws. Yeshua kept the commandments, He followed His father's laws, He loved, He was without sin, He was obedient unto death.

Romans 12:1-2

> *"Therefore brothers, in view of God's mercy, offer your bodies as a living sacrifice — holy and pleasing to the Lord — this is your reasonable, spiritual act of worship. <u>Do not conform any longer to the patterns of this world</u> but be*

*transformed with the renewing of your mind, then you will be able to test and approve of what God's will is - His good, pleasing and perfect will."*

We have many laws in our lives; rules at work, laws of the road, laws of the land, rules in our homes. Many of these are to safeguard us and others. When our children are growing up, we set in place boundaries to protect them, to teach them morals and good behaviour and the right ways of living. Without rules and laws in our lives, we would run amok. We can see that with the loosening of laws in schools and society today, we are becoming a more perverse and dangerous world. Yahweh's laws were put in place for our welfare. Is it now okay to murder, to abort babies? Is it now okay to tell lies, even little white lies? Is it now okay to commit adultery? It must be okay, because the Sabbath has been done away with, right? You throw out one commandment, so we must throw out all of them, right? If anything, Yeshua has added commands to the original law! He has given us a higher standard. Have a look at these next Scriptures that Yeshua spoke to the people:

Matthew 5:21-22

> *"You have heard that it was said to the people long ago, 'You shall not murder, and anyone who murders will be subject to judgment.' But I tell you that anyone who is angry with a brother or sister will be subject to judgment. Again, anyone who says to a brother or sister, 'Raca', is answerable to the court. And anyone who says, 'You fool!' will be in danger of the fire of hell".*

Matthew 5:27-28

> *"You have heard that it was said, 'You shall not commit adultery.' But I tell you that anyone who looks at a woman lustfully has already committed adultery with her in his heart."*

It certainly makes for uncomfortable reading having this higher standard.

It is exciting to note that in the end-time book of Revelation, when the heavens were opened, John could see within Yahweh's heavenly temple and observed the ark of the covenant. We know from Scripture, Hebrews 9:4, that the 10 commandments were placed in the ark of the covenant. I'd like to suggest that if the 10 commandments were not relevant nor important, then we would not have been shown this picture in Revelation. The ark of the covenant is clearly still important to Yahweh; otherwise, why would He bother to keep it in His temple? Everything has its place with Yahweh, there is always order.

Revelation 11:19

> *"Then God's temple in heaven was opened, and within his temple was seen the ark of his covenant..."*

# 2

# SHABBAT (SABBATH DAY)

I personally look forward to Shabbat, it is a time where I can completely relax and unwind and not feel pressured to do anything. What this looks like to me, is that when the sun goes down, I'll perhaps light candles (welcoming in the Shabbat and thanking the Lord for this time He has given me), which makes the day even more special, as it's not something I usually do.

The Sabbath is a time of relaxation and enjoyment. A time of getting up when I want, listening to music, reading my Bible, going for walks or gathering with other like-minded people, visiting friends, etc. I do not feel restricted by this day. I try and organise my week so that I don't have to go shopping or work on this day and as a result, I genuinely find it quite liberating.

Approximately 1.4 billion people – nearly 20% of the world's population – use the word for Sabbath and the seventh day of the week interchangeably. (www.ucg.org/Bible-study-tools/booklets/ sunset-to-sunset-gods-sabbath-rest/names-for-saturday-in-many-languages-prove-which-day-is-the-true-sabbath)

### Languages where Saturday and Sabbath are synonymous

*(Number of speakers in millions, rounded)*

|  |  |  |
| --- | --- | --- |
| Arabic: | *as-Sabt* | 280 |
| Armenian: | *Shabat* | 6 |
| Bosnian: | *Subota* | 2 |
| Bulgarian: | *Sabota* | 7 |
| Corsican: | *Sàbatu* | >1 |
| Croatian: | *Subota* | 6 |
| Czech: | *Sobota* | 10 |
| Georgian: | *Sabati* | 4 |
| Greek: | *Savvato* | 13 |
| Indonesian: | *Sabtu* | 77 |
| Italian: | *Sabato* | 58 |
| Maltese: | *is-Sibt* | >1 |
| Polish: | *Sobota* | 39 |
| Portuguese: | *Sábado* | 215 |
| Romanian: | *Sambata* | 26 |
| Russian: | *Subbota* | 166 |
| Serbian: | *Subota* | 9 |
| Slovak: | *Sobota* | 5 |
| Slovene: | *Sobota* | 2 |
| Somali: | *Sabti* | 15 |
| Spanish: | *Sabado* | 399 |
| Ukrainian: | *Subota* | 40 |

LANGUAGE DATA GATHERED FROM ABOUTWORLDLANGUAGES.COM

I believe that keeping the Sabbath day of rest is very important to the Lord. Right at the very beginning, Yahweh placed significance on this day. The Sabbath day is when the Lord rested on the seventh day from His work in the creation of this world. He wants us to rest too, for our benefit, to keep this seventh day holy (set apart) unto Him.

Genesis 2:3

> *"And Elohim blessed the seventh day and set it apart, because on it He rested from all His work which Elohim in creating had made."*

The Sabbath is from sundown Friday to sundown Saturday and not Sunday as some believe it to be. Sunday is the first day of the week, not the seventh day. The first chapter of Genesis speaks of the creation of the world and the defining of the day. From day one until day seven, evening and morning came, and the Bible tells us that seven days were created.

Genesis 1:5

> *"And God called the light Day, and the darkness he called Night: and the* **evening** *and the* **morning** *were the first day."*

Genesis 1:14

> *"And God said, "Let there be lights in the vault of the sky to separate the day from the night, and <u>let them serve as signs to mark sacred times, and days and years</u>".*

God, Elohim, blessed the Sabbath and set it apart long before Israel existed, in fact, before even man was created!  It is not a holy day just for the Jews (and Israelites), it is for all man.

When the Israelites came out of Egypt, there was also a "great multitude", people not only from the 12 tribes of Israel.  This multitude included Egyptians and any other people who wanted to leave Egypt - why wouldn't you want to leave, when you had just witnessed a supreme God that could control nature, had the power to destroy, but also be your Saviour?

Exodus 12:37-38

> *"The Israelites journeyed from Rameses to Succoth with about 600,000 men on foot, besides women and children.  And a mixed multitude also went up with them, along with great droves of livestock, both flocks and herds...."*

The Sabbath, otherwise called the "Lord's holy day", is in the top 4 of the 10 commandments as we already know, and it is reemphasised here again, in the book of Exodus.

Exodus 20:8-10

> *"Remember the Sabbath day, to set it apart. Six days you labour, and shall do all your work, but the seventh day is a Sabbath of Yahweh your Elohim. You do not do any work… nor your servant… nor your stranger who is within your gates. For in six days Yahweh made the heavens and the earth, the sea, and all that is in them, and <u>rested the seventh day</u>. Therefore, <u>Yahweh blessed the Sabbath day and set it apart</u>."*

This is a repeat of Genesis 2:3, and clearly emphasised here in Exodus 20:8-10. This Sabbath day of rest is for us to be as a remembrance for the Lord's work in creating the earth and everything in it. He rested. He blessed it and made it holy. Even though this is engrained in the 10 commandments, clearly this was set apart before the exodus. This can only emphasise how important it is to Yahweh to set aside the Sabbath day to rest. Our God created this rest day, the seventh day, this holy day right at the beginning.

Isaiah 58:13-14

> *"If you keep your feet from breaking the Sabbath and from doing as you please on my holy day, if you call the Sabbath a delight and the Lord's holy day honourable, and if you honour it by <u>not going your own way and not doing as you please or speaking idle words</u>, then you will find your joy in the Lord..."*

Oh, to truly have real joy in the Lord, not a bad thing, I reckon?

Yahweh himself, wrote the commandments on stone for Moses to take back down the mountain. Why would God write the Sabbath commandment in stone, with His own finger, speak it with His own voice, only to then change it without even producing a clear biblical reference?

Deuteronomy 5:29

> *"Oh, that their hearts would be inclined to fear me and keep all my commands <u>always</u>, so that it might go well with them and their children <u>forever!</u>"*

There are so many verses which remind us to keep the Sabbath and appointed festivals, this is not just a command for the Jewish people and the rest of the Israelite tribes, it is also for those that believe in Yeshua, the son of the living God, who have been grafted into the olive tree (Romans 11:17-24).

After Yeshua's death, Luke 23:56 tells us that the women, who were close to Yeshua, rested on the Sabbath in obedience to the command. These women were regularly with Yeshua, would He not have told them that after his death it no longer mattered? No, Yeshua did not tell them to stop keeping the Sabbath holy, and He did not tell them to stop resting on this day.

On 7th March AD 321, Constantine the Great, a Roman emperor, known as the first Christian Emperor, made it law in the Roman Empire that everyone was to rest on *Sunday*. Constantine honoured the sun god, Sol Invictus, even after proclaiming that he was a Christian. In fact, Constantine made it a decree, under the penalty of death for the people in his empire to cease work on Dies Solis (the day of the sun), Sunday, and this was the day to now rest.

Dies Solis is a reference to the worship of the sun god Apollo, or Sol the sun.[3]

This meant that if you were a follower of Yeshua and you were caught keeping the Shabbat and any Hebrew writings about Yeshua, your life would have been in great danger.

From this time onward, "we" the church, Roman Catholic and Protestant alike, have kept Sunday as the holy day, even though there is nowhere in the Scriptures to suggest that the church should set this particular day apart.

On Shabbat, we are not to go about and do our usual thing, this is a time to be with the Lord, to commune with fellow brothers and sisters in the Lord, to relax and focus on our God.

1 John 5:3

> *"This is love for God, to obey his commands. And his commands are not burdensome."*

---

[3]   "The Fathers of the Church" - Mike Aquilina Clemens Petersen, "CONSTANTINE THE GREAT AND HIS SONS," Philip Schaff, ed., A Religious Encyclopaedia or Dictionary of Biblical, Historical, Doctrinal, and Practical Theology, 3rd edn., Vol. 1. Toronto, New York & London: Funk & Wagnalls Company, 1894. pp.546-547

This does not mean to say that we can't go out for walks, nor go to BBQ's at other people's homes, no. Keeping Sabbath is not about which day to worship our God, we can worship Yahweh, any and every day of the week. It is about honouring and focusing on Him, resting as He has commanded (for our benefit). Simply put, we do not go about our usual business.

Keeping the commandments is how to prove love, they are not a burden.

If we love Yahweh and want to please Him, then we should endeavour to keep His commands and to be holy as He is holy.

1 Peter 1:15-16

> *"But just as He who called you is holy, so be holy in all you do, for it is written: "Be holy, because I am holy."*

Isaiah 35:8

> *"And there will be a highway called the Way of Holiness. The unclean will not travel it, only those who walk in that Way—and fools will not stray onto it."*

As believers, we need to be set apart from the world, to live by God's standards and not by our own or the world's standard.

Yeshua is the master of the Shabbat (Matthew 12:8). When Yahweh's people enter into His Shabbat (rest), they are connecting with the Messiah. Shabbat is the culmination of the week, where the spiritual man rests and rejuvenates his spirit, soul and body in Messiah.

## *Additional Verses to Ponder:*

Yeshua Himself told the religious leaders that He was "Lord also of the Sabbath" (Mark 2:28). Because Yeshua did all of the work of creation (John 1:3), it was He that blessed the seventh day and rested with Adam on that first Sabbath in Eden.

Hebrews 4:1

> *"Therefore, let us be terrified of the possibility that, even though the promise of entering his rest remains, any one of you might be judged to have fallen short of it;"*

James points out that breaking even one of the Ten Commandments makes us guilty of violating the whole.

James 2:10

> *"For whosoever shall keep the whole law, and yet offend in one point, he is guilty of all".*

Deuteronomy 29:29

> *"The secret things belong to the Lord our God, but the things revealed belong to us and to our children forever, that we may follow all the words of this law."*

Ezekiel 20:12

> *"Moreover also, I gave them my Sabbaths, to be a sign between me and them, that they might know that I am the Lord that sanctify them".*

## *Some Historical Quotes about the Sabbath vs Sunday*

Some of the quotes below are directly out of the Catholic doctrines, and you can see that they are absolutely heretical, as they believe that they are above Yahweh and His Word – reminds one of somebody else who wanted to be above Yahweh, and got kicked out of Heaven!

*"Of course, the Catholic Church claims that the change was her act. And the act is a mark of her ecclesiastical power and authority in religious matters."* C. F. Thomas, Chancellor of Cardinal Gibbons, in answer to a letter regarding the change of the Sabbath, November 11, 1895.

*"The retention of the old pagan name of Dies Solis, for Sunday is, in a great measure, owing to the union of pagan and Christian sentiment with which the first day of the week was recommended by Constantine to his subjects - pagan and Christian alike - as the 'venerable' day of the sun."* Arthur P. Stanley, History of the Eastern Church, p. 184

*"Tradition, not Scripture, is the rock on which the church of Jesus Christ is built."* Adrien Nampon, Catholic Doctrine as Defined by the Council of Trent, p. 157

*"The Pope is of so great authority and power that he can modify, explain, or interpret even divine law".* The pope can modify divine law, since his power is not of man, but of God,

*and he acts as vicegerent of God upon earth.* " Lucius Ferraris, Prompta Bibliotheca, art. Papa, II, Vol. VI, p. 29.

*"The Sun was a foremost god with heathen-dom…The sun has worshippers at this hour in Persia and other lands… There is, in truth, something royal, kingly about the sun, making it a fit emblem of Jesus, the Sun of Justice. Hence the church in these countries would seem to have said, to 'Keep that old pagan name [Sunday]. It shall remain consecrated, sanctified.' And thus, the pagan Sunday, dedicated to Balder, became the Christian Sunday, sacred to Jesus."* William Gildea, Doctor of Divinity, The Catholic World, March 1894, p. 809

*"Sunday is a Catholic institution, and… can be defended only on Catholic principles… From beginning to end of Scripture, there is not a single passage that warrants the transfer of weekly public worship from the last day of the week to the first."* Catholic Press, Aug. 25, 1900

*"The Sabbath was Saturday, not Sunday. The Church altered the observance of the Sabbath to the observance of Sunday. Protestants must be rather puzzled by the keeping of Sunday, when God distinctly said, 'Keep holy the Sabbath Day.' The word Sunday does not come anywhere in the Bible, so, without knowing it, they are obeying the authority of the Catholic Church."* Canon Cafferata, The Catechism Explained, p. 89.

*"Deny the authority of the Church, and you have no adequate or reasonable explanation or justification for the substitution of Sunday for Saturday in the Third - Protestant Fourth - Commandment of God... The Church is above the Bible, and this transference of Sabbath observance is proof of that fact."* Catholic Record, September 1, 1923.

*"You are a protestant, and yet you profess to by the Bible and the Bible only; and yet in so important a matter as the observance of one day in seven as a holy day, you go against the plain letter of the Bible, and put another day in the place of that day which the Bible has commanded. The command to keep holy the seventh day is one of the Ten Commandments; you believe that the other nine are still binding; who gave you authority to tamper with the fourth? If you are consistent with your own principles, if you really follow the Bible and the Bible only, you ought to be able to produce some portion of the New Testament in which this fourth commandment is expressly altered."* - The Library of Christian Doctrine, pages 3, 4.

*"The Torah is the Tree of Life! Stop the silly arguments about whether it should be obeyed or not! It is for the REDEEMED of YHWH…not the unredeemed! Yeshua having fulfilled it certainly did not 'do away with it' nor 'nailed it to the stake' nor 'changed it' in any form! He redeemed us from our inherent sinful nature we were born into (slavery to sin) and showed us exactly how we should live as REDEEMED sons and daughters set apart for YHWH! You cannot separate one from the other. Yeshua said, "If you love me, you will obey my commandments." Love is the operative word here, not salvation! Only YHWH saves/redeems through Yeshua, so if you are saved/redeemed by trusting in Yeshua, then you will desire with every fibre of your spirit, soul and body to obey His instructions for life (Torah) out of love and gratitude. Shalom to all who love Him enough to want to obey Him."* Gabi Gildenhuys, 2016.

**3**

# CLEAN AND UNCLEAN FOODS (DIETARY LAWS)

Yahweh had good reasons why animals were defined as clean or unclean. Certain animals in our western mindset are seen as food whereas, in the Torah and Hebrew mindset, the unclean animals were <u>never</u> seen as food. Most unclean animals carry parasites, disease and are extremely high in toxicity. We know from science that high acidity can cause cancer, many of these unclean animals have high acidity. Rabbits, for example, are coprophagous, meaning they eat their own faeces, and the levels of toxins in their bodies are much higher than is acceptable for human consumption.

The Torah gives us good guidelines for healthy eating for valid reasons. I have heard unclean animals described as the "vacuum cleaners for the earth," and I think that suits these animals well. We know that pigs hoover up dead things (including their own kind) and faeces. We know that pigs have very high levels of parasites (worms). Pigs do not have sweat glands, and we know that sweat glands help our bodies to detoxify. Many of the toxins found in pigs are not neutralised by high heat during the cooking process. Scientists backtracked the 2009 swine flu virus (H1N1) outbreak as originating from, yes, you guessed it, swine (pig)! The 2009 swine flu virus caused between 151,700 and 575,400 deaths throughout the world[4].

"Pigs are known to be primary carriers of the following pathogenic organisms, which can create very serious health problems:

- *Taenia solium* tapeworm
- PRRS (Porcine Reproductive and Respiratory Syndrome)

---

[4] **Source:** Dawood, F. S., Iuliano, A.D., Reed, C., et al. Estimated global mortality associated with the first 12 months of 2009 pandemic influenza A H1N1 virus circulation: a modelling study. Lancet Infect Dis. 2012 Jun 26. [Online First]

http://thelancet.com/journals/laninf/article/piis1473-3009(12)70121-4/abstract

- Nipah virus
- Menangle virus
- Hepatitis E virus (HEV)

A *Consumer Reports* investigation found that 69% of all raw pork samples tested, were contaminated with high amounts of volatile microorganisms, such as *Yersinia enterocolitica*. This bacteria causes fever and gastrointestinal stress, and could potentially cause a fatal infection." Dr David Jockers[5].

Dr Mercola states in an article written in July 2016, that "bacon is, in fact, one of the worst types of processed meats you could eat for your health. According to a 2006 study, published in the *American Journal of Clinical Nutrition*, eating bacon five or more times a week, was linked to increasing your risk of bladder cancer by 59 percent. Aside from the processing of the meat, another likely cause for bacon's negative influence on your health, is the heterocyclic amines that form when meat is cooked at high temperatures."[6]

---

[5]    **Source:** Why I Don't Eat Pig Meat - Drjockers.com,
https://drjockers.com/dont-eat-pig-meat/
[6]    **Source:** Are There Deadly Superbugs In Your Pork? - Mercola.com.
        Retrieved from
https://articles.mercola.com/sites/articles/archive/2008/07/12/are-there-deadly-

So, scientifically, we can see that pigs are not good for our health and unsurprisingly, pigs are deemed unclean by Yahweh. So why would we want to eat pork (pig meat)?  Of course, it is not just pork, it is also shellfish, rabbit and hare, amongst other animals and creatures, that are deemed unclean.

Although pork has increased in popularity, is it really too difficult to forego bacon, ham, etc. for the sake of our health and for our love for Yeshua, and replace it with lamb, beef, venison, goat or chicken?  There are many types of meat available that are 'good' and 'clean' and ordained by Yahweh.  Just read the Bible for the list of clean and unclean creatures.

Even Noah knew of clean and unclean, and this was well before the exodus from Egypt, and before the 10 commandments were officially written down by Yahweh.  The Bible talks of the animals that Noah was to take into the ark (how many pairs were there?  Not exactly two by two as we are told in Sunday school).

Genesis 7:2-3

> *"You are to take with you seven of every kind of CLEAN animal, a male and its mate, and two of every kind of UNCLEAN animal, a male and its mate, and also seven of every kind of bird of the air,*

*male and female, in order to preserve their offspring on the face of all the earth."*

Going back to Peter's vision in Acts 10, the vision actually has nothing to do with making unclean animals clean; what God has called unclean stays unclean. Peter wasn't initially sure what his vision actually meant, so why would we be any better in interpreting his vision that we have never had? In verse 19, the Spirit said to go with the Gentile men, and in verse 28, Peter himself makes it clear that he should not call any <u>man</u> common or unclean. Man was never created by Yahweh as common and unclean, for Yahweh created man to be holy. Peter is told in verse 15 of Acts 10, "What Elohim has cleansed you do not consider common".

What the Lord has designed to be holy remains holy, and the definition of holy does not change (although what is holy can be desecrated). Likewise, the definition of clean and unclean "foods" does not change.

Yeshua declared all foods to be clean, but unclean "foods" were never viewed as food in His time at all! The foods declared clean are only the foods that Father Yahweh had already said were clean, and therefore could be eaten. Mark 7 is where this is talked about, and it was bread that was defiled by <u>unclean hands</u> - it's not talking about the food itself. We put our modern western mindset onto something that is not modern and not western; pigs, for example, were never considered food.

1 Corinthians 6:19-20

> *"What? Know you not that your body is the temple of the Holy Ghost which is in you, which you have of God, and you are not your own? For you are bought with a price: therefore, glorify God in your body, and in your spirit, which is God's."*

It's not about thanking God and then eating a poisonous tree frog – don't do it, it's not for our benefit!  And we wonder why we get diseases?  Is it because of the food we eat?  Eat like the Gentiles, get diseases of the Gentiles.  God did not create unclean animals to be eaten by man.  In the last days, God still calls swine and mice as detestable.

Isaiah 66:17

> *"Those who consecrate and purify themselves to go into the gardens, following one who is among those who eat the flesh of pigs, rats and other unclean things - they will meet their end together with the one they follow," declares the LORD."*

We know that before Yeshua died, pigs were considered biblically unclean. So then, after he died, was this changed, and have they now been made clean? No! God did not make a mistake with creation.

There are many good, clean, healthy foods that we can eat, it is not too difficult if one changes ones' mindset, for He says that My yoke is easy, and My burden is light. With the Lord's help, it is easily accomplished.

Why then, would God create the other animals, if they are "unclean"?

As nutritionist David Meinz observes:

"Could it be that God, in His wisdom, created certain creatures whose sole purpose is to clean up after the others? Their entire 'calling' may be to act exclusively as the sanitation workers of our ecology. God may simply be telling us that it's better for us believers not to consume the meat of these trash collectors". *Eating by the Book , 1999, p. 225*

To be biblically kosher is not a Jewish thing, it is a God thing. "Be holy as I am holy."

CLEAN
UNCLEAN
Swine's Flesh
Pig/Hog, Ham, Bacon, Pork
ABOMINATION
Icons made by Freepik from flaticon.com

# 4

# APPOINTED TIMES

I'll come straight in with a handful of verses here, before discussing the Appointed Times[7] (Moedim), which are commanded by Yahweh:

Leviticus 23:37

> *"These are <u>the Lord's</u> appointed feasts which you are to proclaim as <u>sacred</u> assemblies for bringing offerings to the Lord..."*

---

7    Pg55 A Family guide to the Biblical Holidays; Appointed Time is translated as Feast.  The Hebrew word for *feasts* is *mow'ed.* Strong's Number Hebrew 04150 mow'ed or mo'ed or mow'adah. Noun.  Meaning: Appointed times, sacred season, set feast, appointed season, appointed meeting, appointed place, appointed sign, tent of meeting.

Leviticus 23:14

> *"…it shall be a statute <u>forever</u> throughout your generations in all your dwellings."*

Leviticus 23:21

> *"… it shall be a statute <u>forever</u> in all your dwellings throughout your generations."*

Leviticus 23:31

> *"Ye shall do no manner of work: it shall be a statute <u>forever</u> throughout your generations in all your dwellings."*

Leviticus 23:41

> *"And ye shall keep it <u>a feast unto the LORD</u> seven days in the year. It shall be a statute <u>forever</u> in your generations: ye shall celebrate it in the seventh month."*

"Forever" is mentioned a lot of times in just a few verses, let alone the rest of Leviticus. Do you think Yahweh is trying to emphasise to us something, is He trying to make a point? What does "forever" mean?

Following is a summary of seven moedim/ appointed times (feasts) of Yahweh, which are agricultural feasts, but also prophetic feasts, pointing to Yeshua, the Messiah.

## *First, Second and Third Appointed Feasts*

The first three appointed feasts follow quickly upon each other, all within nine days. They are often talked about as the Spring feasts (in the Northern Hemisphere).

The biblical year of the religious calendar starts with the first month of Aviv (Exodus 12), and in this month we have **Passover** beginning at twilight on the 14th Aviv, which is generally in April, depending on the moon phase. Passover is a remembrance of the Lord saving the people from Egypt, represented by the lamb being killed and the blood placed on the doorposts to protect the people, the first born, from the angel of death that passed over the kingdom (Exodus 12). Death is the price paid for this freedom. Passover celebrates freedom. On this day one is still permitted to work. The rules for the observance of Passover are given in Exodus 12:1-28, Leviticus 23:4-8, Numbers 9:1-14, Deuteronomy 16:1-8. The festival involves making an animal sacrifice, although this has been discarded since the Temple was destroyed in AD70.

This Passover in Egypt parallels with Yeshua (Jesus) as our Passover lamb. Yeshua was brought up in an observant family that went to Jerusalem every year at

Passover (Luke 2:41). He was crucified in Jerusalem, while the Jews were gathered together for Passover, and He ate the Passover meal with his disciples the night before he died. Now the entire feast is a memorial to our Messiah's death. Yeshua paid the ultimate price with death for our freedom.

On the 15th day of the month of Aviv, is the Lord's **Feast of Unleavened Bread**. For seven days, it is commanded to eat bread made without yeast. On the 1st and 7th days of this commanded feast, one is to meet with others as directed by Yahweh and do no work, and therefore are extra Sabbath days of rest (Leviticus 23:4-8). The unleavened bread pictures our coming out of sin, and Yeshua as our perfect example of a sinless life. In 1 Corinthians 5:7-8 to the Messiah-believing, covenant-keeping congregation, Paul said:

> *"Therefore, purge out the old leaven, that you may be a new lump, since you truly are unleavened. For indeed Christ, our Passover, was sacrificed for us. Therefore, let us <u>keep the feast</u>, not with old leaven, nor with the leaven of malice and wickedness, but with the unleavened bread of sincerity and truth".*

This passage clearly shows Paul teaching that "keeping the Feasts" is not just for the Jews, but also for believers in Yeshua.

The day after the Feast of Unleavened Bread has finished, there is the appointed day called **First Fruits,** where yet again, there is a High Sabbath rest. One is to gather with others and do no work. It is a joyful feast celebrating the resurrection of the righteous. On this day, the priests waved a harvest offering to the Lord, and a one-year-old lamb was prepared and slaughtered as an ascending offering. This parallels with Yeshua being raised from the dead, and who presented the first harvest of Old Testament believers to Yahweh.

Matthew 27:52-53

> *"The tombs broke open, and the bodies of many holy people who had died were raised to life. They came out of the tombs, and after Jesus' resurrection they went into the holy city and appeared to many people."*

1 Corinthians 15:20

> *"But now is Christ risen from the dead, and has become the first-fruits of those who have fallen asleep."*

1 Corinthians 15:23

> *"But each in his order: Christ the first-fruits, afterward those who are Christ's at His coming."*

Without Yeshua's awesome resurrection, our faith would be nigh on worthless. He had to be a willing sacrifice; He had to die on *that* day to become the Passover Lamb; He had to be the First Fruit of the New Harvest of Believers; otherwise, He could not be the Jewish Messiah prophesied of in Scripture. This time of Passover and the Feast of Unleavened Bread is often misconstrued as Easter, though in reality, it is not the same. See the Easter section for more on this.

## *Fourth Appointed Feast*

This feast is known as Pentecost or as **Shavuot** and comes 50 days after First-Fruits. On Shavuot, this day is also a day to meet with others and do no work, an extra Sabbath rest. The priests wave two loaves of bread over the altar in thanksgiving to the abundant harvest (Leviticus 23:15-21). This was also the day that Moses brought down the 10 commandments from Mt Sinai (Exodus 19), and this is also the day, nearly 1500 years later, that the Holy Spirit came down on all the believers gathered in the upper room, after Yeshua's death (Acts 2), and 3000 people were saved (a harvest). A new boldness came upon the disciples and the people. It is a day of new revelations from Yahweh.

## *Fifth Appointed Feast*

We jump now to what is known as the Fall feasts (northern hemisphere), which is a forty day season, to the 1st day of the 7th month, Tishri (September/ October). It is the season for a time of reflection, contemplation, and putting things in order and getting right our relationship with God; a time for looking inward to spiritual growth, but also a time of joy and celebration.

This fifth appointed feast is a day of rest, commemorated with trumpet blasts, and is known as the **Yom Teruah** (Feast of Trumpets) or as Rosh Hoshanah, the Jewish new year. It is a memorial in Leviticus 23, although it doesn't say what for. The people rejoice in grateful remembrance of Yahweh's benefits. Historically, on this day the Israelites inaugurated the king of Israel, regardless of when the King became the ruler - this day was coronation day. This coronation day reflects Yahweh's kingship.

Psalms 98:6

> *"With trumpets and sound of cornet (shofar) make a joyful noise before the Lord, the King".*

Yom Teruah has a lot of prophetic significance; the trumpet blown (shofar/ram's horn) on this day, foreshadows the return of the Lord (1 Thessalonians 4:16-18).  At the sound of the trumpet, the King will come, and the dead in Messiah will rise first.

1 Thessalonians 4:16

> *"For the Lord himself will come down from heaven, with a loud command, with the voice of the archangel and with the trumpet call of God, and the dead in Christ will rise first."*

Perhaps this is the time of year where we should be watching more closely for his return?

The shofar (trumpet) holds a special place and is significant even for today.  They were and are used to announce approaching festivals, special seasons and in signals of war.  They are also among the symbols used in Revelation.  It was sounded to bring Moses up the mountain to receive the commandments (Exodus 19:19-20).  It was blown at the start of a Jubilee year (Leviticus 25:9).  It is a sign of the regathering of dispersed Israel (Isaiah 27:13).  It, excitingly, will be blown by Yahweh himself, with the arrival of our Messiah!

Zechariah 9:14

> *"And the Lord shall be seen over them, and his arrow shall go forth as the lightning: and the Lord God shall blow the trumpet, and shall go with whirlwinds of the south."*

## Sixth Appointed Feast

This day is seen as the holiest day of the year by the Jews and is known as **Yom Kippur** (the Day of Atonement/Day of Judgment). This day is on the 10th day of the 7th month (September/October), and on this day one is to fast (to afflict one's body) and to make atonement for any wrongdoing in our lives and also for the nations' sin (Leviticus 23:27-32). Yom Kippur is a holy day of the Lord, and remains "a statute forever" and "for the generations to come", a Sabbath day of rest. It is a very serious day of fasting, cleansing, repentance, forgiveness and reflection, and it is also an opportunity to thank Yahweh for His sons' sacrifice. Fasting is not done to rebuke oneself, but to focus on the occasion. It is believed that prophetically speaking, on Yom Kippur, the Lord will judge the people of this world upon His return.

## *Seventh Appointed Feast*

This feast is more like a celebration, a big festival, and is known as the Feast of Tabernacles or **Sukkot,** and it commences on the 15th day of the 7th month (September/October) when the fruit of the land is gathered in. The first and eighth days of this feast are another day to meet with the Lord as directed and are days of rest and rejoicing. The whole week is to be a joyful celebration of Yahweh's provision, care and guidance, and it is usually celebrated outdoors. The people, even today, build sukkahs (temporary dwellings) outside. This ranges from lavish tents with lights to simple branches. It is custom to sleep out under the stars in the sukkah at this time. This feast is also associated with the cloud of glory that covered and protected the people as they moved out of Egypt during the exodus.

Prophetically speaking, this week is a regathering of the exiles to Israel who have been scattered, and is also representative of the bridegroom returning for his bride. This week is also believed by many to be when Yeshua was most likely born.

## *Yeshua and the Feasts (Moedim) and the End Times*

Yeshua was crucified on Passover, buried a moment before Unleavened Bread, raised on First Fruits, and His Holy Spirit, the comforter, came on Shavuot/Pentecost.

The fifth to seventh moedim have not yet been prophetically fulfilled, but they will be at Yeshua's second coming. The moedim are like a wedding rehearsal in anticipation for when the groom arrives for the main event. In Matthew 25:1-13, Yeshua tells the parable of the ten maidens who went out to meet their bridegroom. Five were completely ready and were wise in their preparation, and five were not. They all knew that the bridegroom was coming, but the bridegroom took his time. When He finally came, the foolish (ill-prepared) maidens were left out of the wedding celebrations – they missed out. In verse 13, after Yeshua tells this parable, He commands us to "Watch…". He then immediately continues with another parable about a Master and his servants and the talents to emphasise his point about being diligent with what has been given to us from the Master (Yahweh), and not to be caught out and unaware of His return, so that we are not left out and separated.

We are commanded to keep watch, and we should be even more alert at this time of year for His impending return. How do we know when His return could be if we don't follow His moedim?

1 Thessalonians 5:1-4

> *Now about the times and seasons, brothers, we do not need to write to you. For you are fully aware that the Day of the Lord will come like a thief in the night. While people are saying, "Peace and security," destruction will come upon them suddenly, like labour pains on a pregnant woman, and they will not escape.*
>
> *But you, brothers, are not in the darkness so that this day should overtake you like a thief. For you are all sons of the light and sons of the day; we do not belong to the night or to the darkness.*

Revelation 3:3

> *Remember, then, what you have received and heard. Keep it and repent. If you do not wake up, I will come like a thief, and you will not know the hour when I will come upon you.*

On deeper reflection of these verses, one can clearly see that if we are awake and not in darkness, then we will be aware of when this time will come.

Note that while there is no temple in Jerusalem at this present time, the time will come when the temple will be rebuilt, and animal sacrifices will start again. This will be another sign of Yeshua's imminent return, and very soon after that!

Matthew 24:15

> *"So, when you see standing in the holy place 'the abomination that causes desolation', spoken of through the prophet Daniel - let the reader understand - then let those who are in Judea flee to the mountains."*

Matthew 24:30

> *"At that time the sign of the Son of Man will appear in the sky, and all the nations of the earth will mourn."*

If we count up the actual "rest" days over and above the Sabbath days, there are seven additional rest days throughout the year. These are a blessing designed, not only to honour the Lord, but for us to rest and rest in His presence, a holiday (holy day), one may say, and a glimpse of eternity.

GOD'S HOLY DAYS ARE ALL ABOUT
# MESSIAH YESHUA!

| | |
|---|---|
| PASSOVER | HE DIES |
| UNLEAVENED BREAD | HE RIDS HIS HOUSE OF SIN |
| FIRST FRUITS | HE RAISES FROM THE DEAD |
| PENTECOST | HE SENDS HIS SPIRIT |
| TRUMPETS | HE RETURNS |
| DAY OF ATONEMENT | HE JUDGES THE EARTH |
| TABERNACLES | MARRIAGE SUPPER OF THE LAMB! |

## PRAISE YHVH! (GOD!)

# 5

# FUTURE PROPHETIC SCRIPTURES

We will be keeping His moedim in the future when our Messiah returns as King, not "Jewish" feasts as the world tends to think and say. This is also evidenced in Zechariah 14:16-17

> *"Then it will come about that any who are left of all the nations that went against Jerusalem will go up from year to year to worship the King, the LORD of hosts, and to celebrate the Feast of Tabernacles. And it will be that whichever of the families of the earth does not go up to Jerusalem to worship the King, the LORD of hosts, there will be no rain on them".*

This clearly shows that <u>all</u> the nations will celebrate the Feast of Tabernacles, not just the Israeli people. Why would the people be commanded to celebrate the Feast of Tabernacles during Old Testament days, before our Messiah's death, then with His death, commanded not to keep it,  only to be commanded again to celebrate it, when the Lord returns?  This is inconsistent.

Isaiah 66:23

*"From one new moon to another and from one Sabbath to another, all mankind will come and bow down before me," says the Lord."*

The last chapter in the book of Malachi talks about the Day of the Lord (which hasn't come to pass yet in case there is any doubt) and Yahweh specifically asks us to remember His laws and decrees given to Moses. It's pointless having to remember something unless action is required.

Malachi 4:4

*"<u>Remember</u> the law of my servant Moses, the decrees and laws I gave him at Horeb for all Israel."*

In what we know as the 'end times' (eschatology) book of Revelation, we can see that it is those who remain patient and endure, who remain faithful to Yeshua, and this also includes those who keep His commands - they are not mutually exclusive. Note the "and" in the following verse; there are two specific action points made here.

Revelation 14:12

> *"This calls for patient endurance on the part of the people of God* **who keep his commands _and_ remain faithful to Jesus.** *"*

In Ezekiel's Millennial temple when the Lord has returned, we will be keeping the Sabbath and His appointed times.

Ezekiel 44:15

> *"These Levites and the sons of Tsadoq who guarded the duty of His set-apart place and even when the Israelites went astray, it will be they who will be allowed to serve Yahweh in the innermost courts."*

And Ezekiel 44:23-24 these same people...

> *"...are to teach My people the difference between the set-apart and the profane, and make them know what is unclean and clean. And they are to stand as judges in a dispute and judge it according to My right rulings. And*

*they are to guard My Torah and My laws in all My appointed festivals, and set apart My Sabbaths."*

It is clear from the Scriptures above that we will be keeping Sabbath, the appointed days and the commandments in the future; we will be taught the difference between the profane and the holy, the unclean and the clean, so we can adhere to His rulings and righteous living.

# 6

# TIMES AND SEASONS – HAVE THEY CHANGED?

We know that the anti-Christ will try and change the times and seasons, as told by Daniel in the book of Daniel; perhaps this has already happened? After all, we have different names for the days of the week: pagan, god-worshipping names and names of the months named after Roman gods. As already discussed, we know that in the Torah Yahweh's day of the week starts at sundown, not midnight and that Yahweh's month goes by the moon, not our Gregorian calendar year; the church has "their Sabbath" on a Sunday, and not Saturday (the seventh day).

We know that Passover and Easter are not the same. We know that Yeshua wasn't really born on 25th December.

There is strong evidence to suggest that Yeshua was born between 4 and 6BC and not 1AD as more commonly thought, due to Herod's death in 2BC (note that there were two King Herod's). If this is the case, then our Gregorian calendar is incorrect. We know that there have been a handful of different calendars throughout the centuries.

Daniel prophesied about the change of times and seasons (appointed times).

Daniel 7:25

> *"He will speak against the Most High and oppress his holy people and try to change the set times and the laws. The holy people will be delivered into his hands for a time, times and half a time."*

Could these "set times and laws" that try to be changed, indeed be Yahweh's appointed Holy days and commandments (Sabbath day and moedim) that I discussed earlier? The spirit of the antichrist is so deceptive. We know that Satan is the great deceiver, a liar and a smooth talker and he can make it all look so appealing.

# 7

# CHRISTMAS

There is absolutely no precedent set in the Bible for celebrating Jesus's birth, and no commandment specific to remembering the Messiah's birth.

So, if we want to celebrate His birth, why do we not celebrate Yeshua's birth at the time thought more likely, instead of the 25th December? There are strong clues in the Bible as to the time when Yeshua would have been born. A starting point, with a bit of additional research, can be found in Luke chapter 1, but we will not discuss this here. There are good teachings, available online, that look at this subject. Christmas day is not a mandated feast day, it is not a holy day, and nowhere in the Bible is there any suggestion to keep this day special, but we are told to remember His death.

Even the three wise men (how many? There is actually no number given in the Bible) did not arrive and worship on Yeshua's birthday. They arrived when he was a toddler, approximately two years after the Messiah's birth, following what is known as the Bethlehem Star. Yeshua was not a baby in the manger, as is liked to be portrayed, hence why Herod killed all baby boys two years and younger. The shepherds would not have been out in the fields at night if it was in winter, i.e. 25th December in the northern hemisphere; it would have been too cold even in Israel, and that I can personally testify to.

Are we setting aside the commandments of God in order to keep a tradition?

I can't help but think of the time when Moses was on one of his trips up Mt Sinai (Horeb) with Yahweh, and the people grew impatient and thought their mediator was perhaps dead. What did they do? They thought they needed another mediator to speak with God, and so they built an idol, a golden calf. We know Aaron declared a feast for Yahweh in front of the golden calf (Exodus 32:5-6). They knew the power of God, the people had seen it with their own eyes, they hadn't forgotten the power of Yahweh. I'm sure it was still very fresh in their minds, their miraculous exodus from Egypt, but "Egypt" was still in them, they hadn't completely come out. The people were still holding onto what they had known for over 400 years and were comfortable and familiar with. They were sincere in that they wanted to worship Yahweh, but they wanted to worship Yahweh their way. They unwittingly committed spiritual adultery by breaking not only the first and second, but also the seventh commandment (Exodus 20).

Are we holding on to what is familiar and comfortable? Are we doing this with Christmas? Are we following the traditions of man? The Lord wants us to put Him first.

We need to be careful about what "truths" we are teaching our children. Why do we blur the truth? Why do we mix Santa/Father Christmas with Jesus? We have been warned in the Bible about such things. We are to imitate the Lord and what He did. He never said to remember His birth, only Passover, His death.

Jeremiah 10:2-4

> *"Thus says the LORD: "Learn not the way of the nations, nor be dismayed at the signs of the heavens because the nations are dismayed at them, for the customs of the peoples are vanity. A tree from the forest is cut down and worked with an axe by the hands of a*

*craftsman. They decorate it with silver and gold; they fasten it with hammer and nails so that it cannot move."*

James 4:4

*"You adulterous people! Do you not know that friendship with the world is enmity with God? Therefore, whoever wishes to be a friend of the world makes himself an enemy of God."*

Mixing the ways of the nations and participating in pagan traditions dishonours our Creator.

2 Corinthians 6:15-17

*"What harmony is there between Christ and Belial? Or what does a believer have in common with an unbeliever? What agreement is there between the temple of God and idols? For we are the temple of the living God. As God has said: "I will live with them and walk among them, and I will be their God, and they will be my people. Therefore, "Come out from them and be separate, says the Lord. Touch no unclean thing, and I will receive you."*

Other gods had their birthdays on 25th December, e.g. Mithra, who was a god of light and sacred contracts, was believed to be born out of a rock on 25th December.

"Mithra was an embodiment of the sun, so this period of its rebirth was a major day in Mithraism, which had become Rome's latest official religion… It is believed that the emperor Constantine adhered to Mithraism up to the time of his conversion to Christianity. He was probably instrumental in seeing that the major feast of his old religion was carried over to his new faith." (*The Christmas Almanac, 1979, pg17*)

Yes, it is lovely that it is the one time of year, perhaps two, counting Easter, where Christians feel they can step out and invite people to church, and send a Scripture on a Christmas card. But really, we should be proclaiming the gospel and making disciples throughout the year in our daily lives. It is a sad reflection on Christendom that people only have the boldness and confidence to do this on these occasions, and how effective is it actually? Many believe that it is sowing seeds, but we need to sow seeds throughout the year, in season and out of season, and keep watering them.

2 Timothy 4:2-5

*"Preach the word! Be ready in season and out of season. Convince, rebuke, exhort, with all longsuffering and teaching. 3 For the time will come when they will not endure sound doctrine, but according to their own desires,*

*because they have itching ears, they will heap up for themselves teachers; 4 and they will turn their ears away from the truth, and be turned aside to fables. 5 But you be watchful in all things, endure afflictions, do the work of an evangelist, fulfil your ministry."*

I detest the commercialisation of Christmas; I have never been comfortable with this. The lead up to Christmas is often stressful. The following is a media release by Women's Refuge[8]:

### Women's Refuge says Christmas time not so festive for many families

Media Release 14th December 2016

Women's Refuge is calling on New Zealanders to be more vigilant this Christmas and to think about supporting the many families across NZ affected by family violence. Last year over the holiday season there were over 6000 women and children across Aotearoa that needed Women's Refuge's help, up nearly 30% from the previous Christmas. With their resources already under pressure, Women's Refuge is

---

8    Source: Christmas Time Not So Festive For Many Families | Scoop News.  Retrieved from
http://www.scoop.co.nz/stories/PO1612/S00186/christmas-time-not-so-festive-for-m

hoping that this trend doesn't continue this season. "Christmas can be a particularly volatile time for family violence where we see a significant spike in the numbers of women and children needing our help; this can range from a safe place to sleep, to providing a gift for children to open on Christmas day," says Chief Executive of Women's Refuge Dr Ang Jury.

"We are continually seeing families displaced by family violence over the festive season. There is added pressure with finances, the influence of alcohol, family staying; all of these things can see a high-tension environment turn violent quickly."

Statistically, violence increases, suicides increase, domestic violence significantly increases, alcohol abuse significantly increases, families go into debt just to provide a lavish meal and succumbing to the pressure to buy presents. It is a time of gluttony and over-indulgence. Is that what God wants? Is He in all that? Christmas is not about what it means to us, the questions should really be, *"How does Yahweh see Christmas? What does it mean to Him?"*

Christmas is a form of idolatry disguised with an appearance of holiness to the Lord. The focus is not truly on Him. When the Lord returns, this day will be no more and will be cast aside. This is not one of the Lord's Holy feast days. It is like a wolf in sheep's clothing, an appearance of godliness, but rotten within, deceptive, without good fruit.

The following is quoted from David J. Meyer.[9]

## The True Meaning of Christ-Mass

They tell us that it is the season to be jolly. It is a time of ornaments, red and green decorations, silver bells, holly, mistletoe and coloured lights. It is also a time of department store Santas calling out their universal mantra, "Ho ho ho, Merry Christmas." Nearly all of the realm of so-called "Christianity" join in and repeat this same greeting, "Merry Christmas!"

Although we hear these words constantly, as they resonate millions of times throughout the land, almost nobody understands what they are really saying. It is the purpose of this tract to take the words, "Merry Christmas" and examine the true meaning and essence of those words.

A true Christian would want to examine everything they say, because Jesus said in

---

[9]    **Source**: *The True Meaning Of Christ-mass - Last Trumpet Ministries.* Retrieved from http://www.lasttrumpetministries.org/tracts/tract4.html

Matthew 12:36-37, "But I say unto you, that every idle word that men shall speak, they shall give account thereof in the day of judgement. For by thy words thou shalt be justified, and by thy words, thou shalt be condemned." We will now set aside all of the customs, glitter and traditions of Christmas, which were taken from pagan witchcraft and popularized by the Roman Catholic Church, and we will focus on the true meaning of the words, "Merry Christmas!"

The word "Merry" is simple to define. It unquestionably means to be happy, joyful and light-hearted. The word "merry" fits into the ambience of laughter and frivolity. This word "merry" by itself is innocent and innocuous enough, but as we will now see, it becomes heinously blasphemous when used with the word "Christmas."

Here let it be noted that most people think that the word, "Christmas" means "the birth of Christ." By definition, it means "death of Christ", and I will prove it by using the World Book Encyclopedia, the Catholic Encyclopedia, and a book entitled, The Mass In Slow Motion.

If you are an honest, sincere and discerning Christian, please read on; if not, you might as well stop right here. The World Book

Encyclopedia defines "Christmas" as follows: "The word Christmas comes from "Cristes Maesse", an early English phrase that means "Mass of Christ." (1) It is interesting to note that the word "Mass", as used by the Roman Catholics, has traditionally been rejected by the so-called Protestants, such as Lutherans, Baptists, Methodists, Presbyterians, Pentecostals and so on. The word "Mass" is strictly a Catholic word and thus, so is "Christ-Mass."

It would stand to reason, that since all of these denominations love and embrace "Christ-Mass", that December 25th is the great homecoming day, when all of the Protestants become Catholic for a day. It would seem that all of the so-called "wayward daughters" of the Romish church return to their mother, the scarlet harlot. Thus, all of the so-called Protestant churches could sing to the Pope that popular song "I'll be home for Christmas."

As previously stated, the word "Mass" in religious usage means a "death sacrifice." The impact of this fact is horrifying and shocking; for when the millions of people are saying, "Merry Christmas", they are literally saying "Merry death of Christ!" Furthermore, when the fat man in the red suit laughs boisterously and says, "Ho ho ho, Merry Christmas", he is mocking and laughing at the suffering and bleeding Saviour, who died for our sins. He does this while parents place their little children into his waiting arms to hear his false promises of gifts that he says he will give them. Consider what you are saying when you say, "Merry Christmas."

What is so amusing about our Saviour's painful death? What is so funny? Why is Santa laughing? Why are you going along with it? Your words do count, and Satan knows it. Yes, the word "Mass" does mean "death sacrifice", and to cement that fact, we will consider the definition of the inventors of the religious application of the word "Mass." I am looking at page 537 of the Catholic Encyclopedia, which says, "In the Christian law, the supreme sacrifice is that of the Mass." It goes on to say, "The supreme act of worship consists essentially in an offering of a worthy victim to God, the offering made by a proper person, as a priest, the destruction of the victim." (2) Please note carefully the word, "victim" of the Mass. The Latin word for victim is "Hostia" from which the word "host" is derived. The Mass, by definition of those who coined the word, is a sacrifice involving a victim. There is no other meaning for the word "Mass" or "Christ-Mass." On page 110 of a book entitled "The Mass In Slow Motion", we find the following words: "It is only with the consecration that the sacrifice of the Mass is achieved.  I have represented the Mass to you, more than once, as a kind of ritual dance." (3)

In essence, the Mass is the ceremonial slaying of Jesus Christ over and over again, followed by the eating of his flesh and the drinking of his blood.  The Mass is the death sacrifice, and the "Host" is the victim.  This is official Roman Catholic doctrine, and "Christmas" is a word that they invented.  Again, I ask, what is so merry about the pain, bleeding, suffering and death of Jesus Christ? Satan has done quite a job of getting millions of so-called "Christians" to blaspheme. What a deceiver he is.

Now you know the true meaning of the word "Christmas" or Mass of Christ. There is much more to know about this pagan holiday, and we will be glad to provide you with plenty of evidence that Jesus was not born on December 25th, and that Christmas is not only a lie, but is actually a witches' sabbat called "Yule" in clever disguise. Please contact us at the address below, and for the sake of your soul, flee from idolatry!

## Acknowledgements:

01. World Book Encyclopedia, vol.3, p. 408, 1986 ed., World Book Inc., Chicago, IL

02. The Catholic Encyclopedia, R.C. Broderick, 1975 ed., Nihil Obstat, Richard J. Sklba, Censor Librorum. Imprimatur, Archbishop William E. Cousins, Milwaukee, WI.

03. The Mass In Slow Motion, Ronald Knox, 1948, Sheed & Ward, Inc., New York, NY. Nihil Obstat, E.C. Messenger, Censor Deputatus. Imprimatur, E. Morrogh Bernard, Vic. Gen.

Last Trumpet Ministries International

PO Box 806

Beaver Dam, WI 53916, U.S.A.

The following excerpt is by Lawrence Kelemen and is quite a lengthy but interesting article on the history of Christmas. In this article, CE and BCE refer to Current Era, and Before Current Era. These are modern references to what in other areas of my book is referred to, and traditionally known, as AD (Anno Domini – The year of our Lord) and BC (Before Christ).

## The History of Christmas

I.  **When was Jesus born?**

A.  Popular myth puts his birth on December 25th in the year 1 CE.

B.  The New Testament gives no date or year for Jesus's birth. The earliest gospel – St. Mark's, written about 65 CE– begins with the baptism of an adult Jesus. This suggests that the earliest Christians lacked interest in or knowledge of Jesus's birth date.

C.  The year of Jesus's birth was determined by Dionysius Exiguus, a Scythian monk, "abbot of a Roman monastery". His calculation went as follows:

a.  In the Roman, pre-Christian era, years were counted from *ab urbe condita* ("the founding of the City" [Rome]). Thus 1 AUC signifies the year Rome was founded, 5 AUC signifies the 5th year of Rome's reign, etc.

b.  Dionysius received a tradition that the Roman emperor Augustus reigned 43 years, and was followed by the emperor Tiberius.

c.  Luke 3:1,23 indicates that when Jesus

turned 30 years old, it was the 15th year of Tiberius's reign.

d.  If Jesus was 30 years old in Tiberius's reign, then he lived 15 years under Augustus (placing Jesus' birth in Augustus' 28th year of reign).

e.  Augustus took power in 727 AUC. Therefore, Dionysius put Jesus birth in 754 AUC.

f.  However, Luke 1:5 places Jesus's birth in the days of Herod, and Herod died in 750 AUC – four years *before* the year in which Dionysius places Jesus birth.

D.  Joseph A. Fitzmyer – Professor Emeritus of Biblical Studies at the Catholic University of America, member of the Pontifical Biblical Commission, and former president of the Catholic Biblical Association – writing in the Catholic Church's official commentary on the New Testament, writes about the date of Jesus's birth, "Though the year of Jesus's birth is not reckoned with certainty, the birth did not occur in 1 CE. The Christian era, supposed to have its starting point in the year of Jesus's birth, is based on a miscalculation introduced ca. 533 by Dionysius Exiguus."

E.  The *DePascha Computus*, an anonymous

document believed to have been written in North Africa around 243 CE, placed Jesus's birth on March 28. Clement, a bishop of Alexandria (d. ca. 215 CE), thought Jesus was born on November 18. Based on historical records, Fitzmyer guesses that Jesus's birth occurred on September 11, 3 BCE.

## II. How Did Christmas Come to Be Celebrated on December 25?

A. Roman pagans first introduced the holiday of Saturnalia, a week-long period of lawlessness, celebrated between December 17-25. During this period, Roman courts were closed, and Roman law dictated that no one could be punished for damaging property or injuring people, during the weeklong celebration. The festival began when Roman authorities chose "an enemy of the Roman people" to represent the "Lord of Misrule." Each Roman community selected a victim whom they forced to indulge in food and other physical pleasures throughout the week. At the festival's conclusion, December 25th, Roman authorities believed they were destroying the forces of darkness by brutally murdering this innocent man or woman.

B. The ancient Greek writer, poet and historian Lucian (in his dialogue entitled *Saturnalia*) describes the festival's observance in his time. In addition to human sacrifice, he mentions these customs: widespread intoxication; going from house to house while singing naked; rape and other sexual license; and consuming human-shaped biscuits (still produced in some English and most German bakeries during the Christmas season).

C. In the 4th century CE, Christianity imported the Saturnalia festival hoping to take the pagan masses in with it. Christian leaders succeeded in converting to Christianity large numbers of pagans by promising them that they could continue to celebrate the Saturnalia as Christians.

D. The problem was that there was nothing intrinsically Christian about Saturnalia. To remedy this, these Christian leaders named Saturnalia's concluding day, December 25th, to be Jesus's birthday.

E. Christians had little success, however, refining the practices of Saturnalia. As Stephen Nissenbaum, professor of history at the University of Massachusetts, Amherst, writes, "In return for ensuring massive observance of the anniversary of the Saviour's birth by assigning it to this resonant date, the Church, for its part, tacitly agreed to allow the holiday to be celebrated more or less the way it had always been." The earliest Christmas holidays were celebrated by drinking, sexual indulgence, singing naked in the streets (a precursor of modern carolling), etc.

F. The Reverend Increase Mather of Boston observed in 1687 that "the early Christians, who first observed the Nativity on December 25, did not do so thinking that Christ was born in that Month, but because the Heathens' Saturnalia was at that time kept in Rome, and they were willing to have those Pagan Holidays metamorphosed into Christian ones." Because of its known pagan origin, Christmas was banned by the Puritans, and its observance was illegal in Massachusetts between 1659 and 1681. However, Christmas was and still is celebrated by most Christians.

G. Some of the most depraved customs of the Saturnalia carnival were intentionally revived by the Catholic Church in 1466, when Pope Paul II, for the amusement of his Roman citizens, forced Jews to race naked through the streets of the city. An eyewitness account reports, "Before they were to run, the Jews were richly fed, so as to make the race more difficult for them and at the same time more amusing for spectators. They ran… amid Rome's taunting shrieks and peals of laughter, while the Holy Father stood upon a richly ornamented balcony and laughed heartily."

H. As part of the Saturnalia carnival throughout the 18th and 19th centuries CE, rabbis of the ghetto in Rome were forced to wear clownish outfits and march through the city streets to the jeers of the crowd, pelted by a variety of missiles. When the Jewish community of Rome sent a petition in 1836 to Pope Gregory XVI, begging him to stop the annual Saturnalia abuse of the Jewish community, he responded, "It is not opportune to make any innovation." On December 25, 1881, Christian leaders whipped the Polish masses into anti-Semitic frenzies that led to riots across the country. In Warsaw, 12 Jews were brutally murdered, huge numbers maimed, and many Jewish women were raped. Two million rubles' worth of property was destroyed.

## III. The Origins of Christmas Customs

### A. **The Origin of Christmas Tree**

Just as early Christians recruited Roman pagans by associating Christmas with the Saturnalia, so too, worshippers of the

Asheira cult and its offshoots were recruited by the Church sanctioning "Christmas Trees". Pagans had long worshipped trees in the forest, or brought them into their homes and decorated them, and this observance was adopted and painted with a Christian veneer by the Church.

B. **The Origin of Mistletoe**

Norse mythology recounts how the god Balder was killed using a mistletoe arrow by his rival god Hoder while fighting for the female Nanna. Druid rituals use mistletoe to poison their human sacrificial victim. The Christian custom of "kissing under the mistletoe" is a later synthesis of the sexual license of Saturnalia with the Druidic sacrificial cult.

C. **The Origin of Christmas Presents**

In pre-Christian Rome, the emperors compelled their most despised citizens to bring offerings and gifts during the Saturnalia (in December) and Kalends (in January). Later, this ritual expanded to include gift-giving among the general populace. The Catholic Church gave this custom a Christian flavour by re-rooting it in the supposed gift-giving of Saint Nicholas (see below).

D. **The Origin of Santa Claus**

    a. Nicholas was born in Parara, Turkey

in 270 CE and later became Bishop of Myra.  He died in 345 CE on December 6th.  He was only named a saint in the 19th century.

b.  Nicholas was among the most senior bishops who convened the Council of Nicaea in 325 CE, and created the New Testament.  The text they produced portrayed Jews as "the children of the devil" who sentenced Jesus to death.

c.  In 1087, a group of sailors who idolized Nicholas, moved his bones from Turkey to a sanctuary in Bari, Italy.  There, Nicholas supplanted a female boon-giving deity called The Grandmother, or Pasqua Epiphania, who used to fill the children's stockings with her gifts.  The Grandmother was ousted from her shrine at Bari, which became the centre of the Nicholas cult.  Members of this group gave each other gifts during a pageant they conducted annually, on the anniversary of Nicholas's death, December 6.

d.  The Nicholas cult spread north, until it was adopted by German and Celtic pagans.  These groups worshipped a pantheon led by Woden – their chief god and the father of Thor, Balder, and Tiw. Woden had a long, white beard and rode a horse through the heavens, one evening each Autumn. When Nicholas merged with Woden, he shed his Mediterranean appearance, grew a beard, mounted a flying horse, rescheduled his flight for December, and donned heavy winter clothing.

e. In a bid for pagan adherents in Northern Europe, the Catholic Church adopted the Nicholas cult and taught that he did (and they should) distribute gifts on December 25th, instead of December 6th.

f. In 1809, the novelist Washington Irving (most famous his *The Legend of Sleepy Hollow* and *Rip Van Winkle*) wrote a satire of Dutch culture, entitled *Knickerbocker History*. The satire refers several times to the white-bearded, flying-horse riding Saint Nicholas using his Dutch name, Santa Claus.

g. Dr. Clement Moore, a professor at Union Seminary, read *Knickerbocker History*, and in 1822, he published a poem based on the character Santa

Claus: "'Twas the night before Christmas, when all through the house, not a creature was stirring, not even a mouse. The stockings were hung by the chimney with care, in the hope that Saint Nicholas soon would be there..." Moore innovated by portraying a Santa with eight reindeer who descended through chimneys.

h. The Bavarian illustrator Thomas Nast almost completed the modern picture of Santa Claus. From 1862 through 1886, based on Moore's poem, Nast drew more than 2,200 cartoon images of Santa for *Harper's Weekly*. Before Nast, Saint Nicholas had been pictured as everything from a stern looking bishop to a gnome-like figure in a frock. Nast also gave Santa a home at the North Pole, his workshop filled with elves, and his list of the good and bad children of the world. All Santa was missing was his red outfit.

i. In 1931, the Coca Cola Corporation contracted the Swedish commercial artist Haddon Sundblom to create a coke-drinking Santa. Sundblom modelled his Santa on his friend Lou Prentice, chosen for his cheerful, chubby face. The corporation insisted that Santa's fur-trimmed suit be bright, Coca Cola red. And Santa was born – a blend of Christian crusader, pagan god, and commercial idol.

## IV. The Christmas Challenge

Christmas has always been a holiday celebrated carelessly. For millennia, pagans, Christians, and even Jews have been swept away in the season's festivities, and very few people ever pause to consider the celebration's intrinsic meaning, history, or origins.

Christmas celebrates the birth of the Christian god who came to rescue mankind from the "curse of the Torah." It is a 24-hour declaration that Judaism is no longer valid.

Christmas is a lie. There is no true Christian church with a tradition that Jesus was really born on December 25th.

December 25 is a day on which Jews have been shamed, tortured, and murdered.

Many of the most popular Christmas customs – including Christmas trees, mistletoe, Christmas presents, and Santa Claus – are modern incarnations of the most depraved pagan rituals ever practised on earth.

Many who are excitedly preparing for their

Christmas celebrations, would prefer not knowing about the holiday's real significance. If they do know the history, they often object that their celebration has nothing to do with the holiday's monstrous history and meaning. "We are just having fun."

Imagine that between 1933-45, the Nazi regime celebrated Adolf Hitler's birthday – April 20 – as a holiday. Imagine that they named the day, "Hitlerday," and observed the day with feasting, drunkenness, gift-giving, and various pagan practices. Imagine that on that day, Jews were historically subject to perverse tortures and abuse, and that this continued for centuries.

Now, imagine that your great-great-great-grandchildren were about to celebrate Hitlerday. April 20th arrived. They had long forgotten about Auschwitz and Bergen Belsen. They had never heard of gas chambers or death marches. They had purchased champagne and caviar, and were about to begin the party, when someone reminded them of the day's real history and their ancestors' agony. Imagine that they initially objected, "We aren't celebrating the Holocaust; we're just having a little Hitlerday party." If you could travel forward in time and meet them; if you could say a few words to them, what would you advise them to do on Hitlerday?

On December 25, 1941, Julius Streicher, one of the most vicious of Hitler's assistants, celebrated

Christmas by penning the following editorial in his rabidly Antisemitic newspaper, *Der Stuermer*.

> If one really wants to put an end to the continued prospering of this curse from heaven that is the Jewish blood, there is only one way to do it: to eradicate this people, this Satan's son, root and branch.

It was an appropriate thought for the day. This Christmas, how will we celebrate?


## AUTHOR: LAWRENCE KELEMEN

*Source:* Addison G. Wright, Roland E. Murphy, Joseph A. Fitzmyer, "A History of Israel" in *The Jerome Biblical Commentary*, (Prentice Hall: Englewood Cliffs, NJ, 1990), p. 1247.

The first mention of a Nativity feast appears in the Philocalian calendar, a Roman document from 354 CE, which lists December 25th as the day of Jesus' birth.

Increase Mather, *A Testimony against Several Prophane and Superstitious Customs, Now Practiced by Some in New England* (London, 1687), p. 35.

Stephen Nissenbaum, *The Battle for Christmas: A Cultural History of America's Most Cherished Holiday*, New York: Vintage Books, 1997, p. 4, p. 3.

David I. Kertzer, *The Popes Against the Jews: The Vatican's Role in the Rise of Modern Anti-Semitism*, New York: Alfred A. Knopf, 2001, p. 74, p. 33, 74-5.

Clement Miles, *Christmas Customs and Traditions: Their History and Significance*, New York: Dover Publications, 1976, pp. 178, 263-271, p. 273, p. 274-5.

# 8

# EASTER

We are taught that Yeshua died and rose again at Easter. We are taught that He died on Friday and rose on Sunday. We know He had His "last supper" with His disciples in Jerusalem. We know He was buried and then there was the "preparation day" before the Sabbath rest. We know, as prophesied, that as Jonah was three days and three nights in the fish, so Messiah would be dead three days and three nights.

In accordance with Scripture, Yeshua dying and buried on Friday and rising on Sunday morning, does not equal three days and three nights. Friday night, Saturday night = two nights.

Matthew 12:40

*"For as Jonah was three days and three nights in the belly of a huge fish, so the Son of Man will be three days and three nights in the heart of the earth".*

The Britannica Encyclopedia (1934) states "Easter (es'ter). Ostara, or Eastre, was the goddess of Spring in the religion of the ancient Angles and Saxons. Every April a festival was celebrated in her honour. With the beginnings of Christianity, the old gods were put aside. From then on the festival was celebrated in honour of the resurrection of Christ, but was still known as Easter after the old goddess."

Easter (Ishtar) is the name of a fertility goddess. She is actually known by many different names around the world, including Astarte (Greek), Ashtaroth (Hebrew/Canaanite), Ishtar (Babylonian) and Eastre (Anglo Saxon). Ishtar is but another name for Semiramis, the wife of Nimrod. Nimrod was worshipped as the Sun God, and he and Ishtar instituted the building of the Tower of Babel (read Genesis chapters 10 and 11 for more on Nimrod). Nimrod is also known by a variety of names such as Baal, Moloch and Tammuz, which you will read of in the Bible.

I have come across a website that specifically discusses their god Eostre, and their modern-day rituals at Easter. You will see that their custom is very similar to that of western tradition: Easter eggs, etc. The following is a quote from 2006 by A.E. Hunt-Anschutz:[10]

> "In my own heathen tradition, we see Eostre as a joyful goddess associated with spring and new growth - not because we read that anywhere, but because that's how she comes across to us. We celebrate Eostrefest in April on the first weekend after the bluebells come into bloom. We always hold this festival outdoors in woodland, no matter how rainy or muddy. We have a wooden statue of Eostre which takes centre stage on an altar. Next to it is a plate of seeds.
>
> We start with everyone making food or drink offerings to the wights of the wood. Then we welcome Eostre and give her an offering of mead - splashing it on her statue. We ask the wood wights to bless the seeds for us, so that we can remember them and honour them throughout the summer.
>
> All participants bring an eggcup. We fill these with mead, and then ritually bless them.

---

[10]   **Source**: *Eostre And Easter Customs - Manygods.org.uk.*
Retrieved from http://www.manygods.org.uk/articles/essays/Eostre.shtml

Everyone simultaneously tosses the mead up in the air and yells "Hail Eostre!" - with the goal of getting as much mead raining down on others as possible. Next, we fill a horn with mead and have a round of toasts to Eostre, spring and new growth. Afterwards, we feast (picnicking if the weather permits). Decorated hard-boiled eggs, as well as chocolate eggs, tend to be on the menu. I very much doubt the heathen Anglo-Saxons honoured Eostre with egg cups. I very much doubt they had egg cups. But, all who attend our Eostrefest seem to feel that the goddess approves - and that she gets a kick out of watching us soak each other in mead in her honour."

Jacob Grimm in *Teutonic Mythology* (published 1835), tells us that the Anglo-Saxon name Eostre is related to Old High German adverb *ostar,* expressing movement toward the rising sun. "Ostara, Eostre seems, therefore, to have been a divinity of the radiant dawn, of up-springing light, a spectacle that brings joy and blessing, whose meaning could be easily adapted to the resurrection-day of the Christian's God."

It is on the summer solstice (northern hemisphere) when pagans worship their gods. The rabbit and the egg are symbols of fertility goddess worship, and it is said that the painted eggs were originally dipped in the blood of babies that were sacrificed! Hot cross buns are said to be the raised cakes that were baked for Ishtar, the Queen of Heaven.

Jeremiah 7:18

> *"The children are gathering wood, the fathers are lighting the fire, and the women are kneading their dough, to make cakes for the Queen of Heaven, and to pour out drink offerings to other mighty ones, to provoke Me.*

Jeremiah 44:19

> *"And when we burned incense to the Queen of Heaven and poured out drink offerings to her, did we make cakes for her, to idolize her…"*

By contrast, our Creator says:

Deuteronomy 12:3-4

> *"Break down their altars, smash their sacred stones and burn their Asherah poles in the fire; cut down the idols of their gods and wipe out their names from those places. You must not worship the Lord your God in their way."*

I don't want to dwell on the other gods, except to highlight that our Easter is not so much "ours" and that this celebration of death, resurrection and new life, is not all that it seems. The bible does not mention anything about Easter eggs, Easter baskets or bunnies, it does not even mention Lent. This too, is like a wolf being hidden in the appearance of a sheep. Indeed, Easter is not unlike the golden calf incident that we discussed earlier. Again, are we worshipping God His way or our way?

We are commanded to keep Passover.

Let me be very clear, Easter is not Passover.

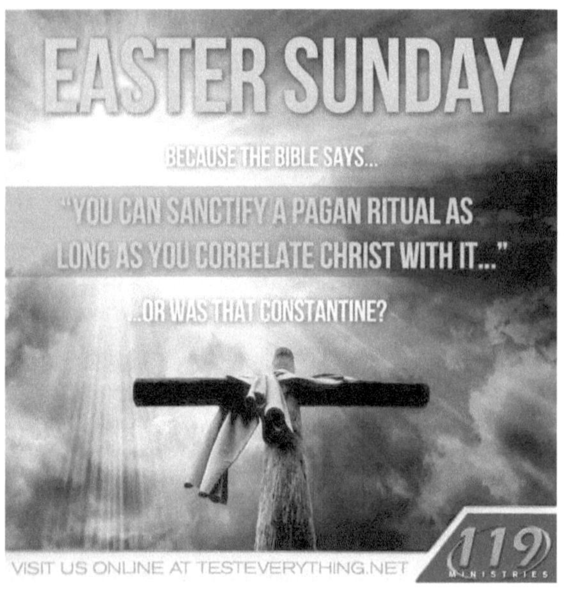

# 9

# SUMMARY

So, we have the argument: What about Colossians 2:16-17: *"Therefore let no one judge you by what you eat or drink, or with regard to a festival, a New Moon, or a Sabbath. These are a shadow of the things to come, but the body that casts it belongs to Christ."*

Does this mean that we are no longer required to keep the Ten Commandments of the "Old Testament"? Does this mean that all of what God commanded the Israelites, is therefore abolished, by one letter Paul wrote to one group of Believers?

Firstly, you have to consider what was going on and who the letter was addressed to and who wrote it. Paul wrote it in a letter to the Church of Colossae. At the time that this congregation of Believers was established, they were more than likely meeting on the Sabbath, as did all true Believers. The city was infiltrated with false teachings. So, who was being judged? The church was, because they were different, meaning that they ate different meat and drank differently. They respected different holy days and observed the phases of the moon, rather than the sun, and all of this was different from the world around them.

So, what Paul was really saying to this congregation of Believers, was, "Don't let anybody judge you because you are following God's commands, by only eating clean foods, observing God's Sabbath, and celebrating God's appointed Feasts, that are timed according to the moon phases and not the sun."

The second thing to note is that in Revelation 12:17, it states very clearly:

> *"And the dragon was enraged at the woman, and went to make war with the rest of her children, who keep the commandments of God and hold to the testimony of Jesus."*

So, according to this verse, it's those who ARE keeping the commands of Yahweh, and following Yeshua, whom the enemy is going after.

Ultimately, Yahweh's law, Yahweh's Word, and our faith is all about love: Yahweh's love for us to keep us from harm, and our love for Him, outworking in obedience to His ways. Love is a verb, a "doing" word, an action.

Thankfully, we do have the Lord's grace and mercy and compassion, and thankfully, He is slow to anger. Thankfully too, Yahweh is a forgiving God and always has been.

Without all this, it would be impossible, but we know that in Him all things are possible, and He strengthens us to walk in His will, to keep His commands.

In the parable of the ten virgins, all of them knew the groom (Yeshua) was coming one day soon, they were all "believers" in Yeshua. But five were foolish and not 100% ready, only a little bit ready, but that was not enough. They missed out. I don't want to be the bride that misses out.

There will come a time (and soon) where enough is enough, and the wrath of Yahweh will come upon this earth, and many will fall. I don't want to fall. I want to be that person that when I, and I alone, stand before my heavenly Father, and when He pronounces judgement, that He will say, "Well done, good and faithful servant." I don't want to hear Him say, "Why didn't you keep my commands when I clearly told you to?". At the end of the day, it is an individual walk with the Lord, and when we stand before the throne of judgment, it will be on our own, not with our spouses or our children. We each have our own walk with the Lord, and we have to work it out in "fear and trembling".

Our job is to adjust our lives to the truth, no matter how difficult it may be. It's not just about being sincere in heart. We still need to line up with the Scriptures and to be obedient. Yeshua has an even higher standard for living than what we see in the Old Testament, the Torah and the Prophets.

The Torah is a reflection of the righteousness of God, of Yahweh, and therefore it cannot be wrong. Just because someone is at fault and has an inability to follow the instructions/Torah, doesn't mean to say that the Torah is at fault.

The ancient way as described in Jeremiah 6:16, is the good way; it is still very much important, and perhaps even more so, as the world moves away from the things of God and the people lose their moral compass.

*"Thus says Yahweh, "Stand at the crossroads and look; and ask after the <u>ancient path</u>, where the good way is, and walk in it. <u>And you will find rest for your souls</u>. But they said we will not walk in it..."*

And remember, in Matthew 5:17-19, Yeshua says "...Until heaven and earth disappear, not the smallest letter, nor the least stroke of the pen will disappear from the law until everything has been accomplished. If anyone breaks the least of these commandments and teaches others to do the same, they will be least in the kingdom of heaven..."

Either keeping Sabbath, the commandments and the appointed feasts, are a thing of the past, or they are still relevant for Yahweh and Yeshua's people for today. Which is it? If the Lord is the same yesterday, today and forever (Hebrews 13:8), then there can only be one conclusion: YAHWEH's laws are still valid for today and should be remembered and practised by all those who believe in the Messiah.

John 4:23-24

*"Yet a time is coming and has now come when the true worshipers will worship the Father in the Spirit and in truth, for they are the kind of worshipers the Father seeks. God is spirit, and his worshipers must worship in the Spirit and in truth."*

Whoever keeps commandments keeps their life,
but whoever shows contempt for their ways will die.
— PROVERBS 19:16 NIV

Image used with permission

# APPENDIX

## *100 Amazing Facts about the Sabbath & Sunday*

WHY keep the Sabbath day? What is the object of the Sabbath? Who made it? When was it made, and for whom? Which day is the true Sabbath? Many keep the first day of the week, or Sunday. What Bible authority have they for this? Some keep the seventh day, or Saturday. What Scripture have they for that? Here are the facts about both days, as plainly stated in the Word of God:

## 60 Bible Facts about the Sabbath or Seventh Day

1. After working the first six days of the week in creating this earth, the great God rested on the seventh day. (Genesis 2:1.3)

2. This stamped that day as God's rest day, or Sabbath day, as Sabbath day means rest day. To illustrate: When a person is born on a certain day, that day thus becomes his birthday. So, when God rested upon the seventh day, that day became His rest, or Sabbath, day.

3. Therefore, the seventh day must always be God's Sabbath day. Can you change your birthday from the day on which you were born to one on which you were not born? No. Neither can you change God's rest day to a day on which He did not rest. Hence the seventh day is still God's Sabbath day.

4. The Creator blessed the seventh day. (Genesis 2:3)

5. He sanctified the seventh day. (Exodus 20:11)

6. He made it the Sabbath day in the Garden of Eden. (Genesis 2:1-3)

7. It was made before the fall; hence it is not a type; for types were not introduced till after the fall.

8. Jesus says it was made for man (Mark 2:27), that is, for the race, as the word man is here unlimited; hence, for the Gentile as well as for the Jew.

9. It is a memorial of creation. (Exodus 20:11; 31:17) Every time we rest upon the seventh day, as God did at creation, we commemorate that grand event.

10. It was given to Adam, the head of the human race. (Mark 2:27; Genesis 2:1-3)

11. Hence through him, as our representative, to all nations. (Acts 17:26)

12. It is not a Jewish institution, for it was made 2,300 years before there ever was a Jew.

13. The Bible never calls it the Jewish Sabbath, but always "the Sabbath of the Lord thy God." Men should be cautious about how they stigmatize God's holy rest day.

14. Evident reference is made to the Sabbath and the seven-day week, all through the patriarchal age. (Genesis 2:1-3; 8:10,12; 29:27-28, etc.)

15. It was a part of God's law before Sinai. (Exodus 16:4, 27-29)

16. Then God placed it in the heart of His moral law. (Exodus 20:1-17) Why did He place it there, if it was not like the other nine precepts, which all admit to being immutable?

17. The seventh-day Sabbath was commanded by the voice of the living God. (Deuteronomy 4:12-13)

18. Then He wrote the commandment with His own finger. (Exodus 31:18)

19. He engraved it in the enduring stone, indicating its imperishable nature. (Deuteronomy 5:22)

20. It was sacredly preserved in the ark, in the holy of holies. (Deuteronomy 10:1-5)

21. God forbade work upon the Sabbath, even in the most hurrying times. (Exodus 34:21)

22. God destroyed the Israelites in the wilderness because they profaned the Sabbath. (Ezekiel 20:12-13)

23. It is the sign of the true God, by which we are to know Him from false gods. (Ezekiel 20:20)

24. God promised that Jerusalem should stand forever if the Jews would keep the Sabbath (Jeremiah 17:24-25)

25. He sent them into the Babylonish captivity for breaking it. (Nehemiah 13:18)

26. He destroyed Jerusalem for its violation. (Jeremiah 17:27)

27. God has pronounced a special blessing on all the Gentiles who will keep it. (Isaiah 56:6-7)

28. This is in the prophecy, which refers wholly to the Christian dispensation. (See Isaiah 56)

29. God has promised to bless all who keep the Sabbath. (Isaiah 56:2)

30. The Lord requires us to call it "honourable". (Isaiah 58:13) Beware, ye who take delight in calling it the "old Jewish Sabbath," "a yoke of bondage," etc.

31. After the holy Sabbath has been trodden down "many generations," it is to be restored in the last days. (Isaiah 58:12-13)

32. All the holy prophets kept the seventh day.

33. When the Son of God came, He kept the seventh day all His life. (Luke 4:16; John 15:10) Thus, He followed His Father's example at creation. Shall we

not be safe in following the example of both the Father and the Son?

34. The seventh day is the Lord's Day. (See Revelation 1:10; Mark 2:28; Isaiah 58:13; Exodus 20:10)

35. Jesus was Lord of the Sabbath (Mark 2:28), that is, to love and protect it, as the husband is the lord of the wife, to love and cherish her. (1 Peter 3:6)

36. He vindicated the Sabbath as a merciful institution, designed for man's good. (Mark 2:23-28)

37. Instead of abolishing the Sabbath, He carefully taught how it should be observed. (Matthew 12:1-13.)

38. He taught His disciples that they should do nothing upon the Sabbath day, but what was "lawful". (Matthew 12:12)

39. He instructed His apostles that the Sabbath should be prayerfully regarded forty years after His resurrection. (Matthew 24:20)

40. The pious women who had been with Jesus carefully kept the seventh day after His death. (Luke 23:56)

41. Thirty years after Christ's resurrection, the Holy Spirit expressly calls it "the Sabbath day,"(Acts 13:14)

42. Paul, the apostle to the Gentiles, called it the "Sabbath day" in AD45. (Acts 13:27) Did not Paul know? Or shall we believe modern teachers, who affirm that it ceased to be the Sabbath at the resurrection of Christ?

43. Luke, the inspired Christian historian, writing as late as AD62, calls it the "Sabbath day." (Acts 13:44)

44. The Gentile converts called it the Sabbath. (Acts 13:42)

45. In the great Christian council, AD49, in the presence of the apostles and thousands of disciples, James calls it the "Sabbath day." (Acts 15:21)

46. It was customary to hold prayer meetings upon that day. (Acts 16:13)

47. Paul read the Scriptures in public meetings on that day. (Acts 17:2-3)

48. It was his custom to preach upon that day. (Acts 17:2-3.)

49. The Book of Acts alone gives a record of his holding eighty-four meetings upon that day. (See Acts 13:14, 44; 16:13; 17:2; 18:4, 11.)

50. There was never any dispute between the Christians and the Jews about the Sabbath day. This is proof that the Christians still observed the same day that the Jews did.

51. In all their accusations against Paul, they never charged him with disregarding the Sabbath day. Why did they not, if he did not keep it?

52. But Paul himself expressly declared that he had kept the law. "Neither against the law of the Jews, neither against the temple, nor yet against Caesar, have I offended anything at all." Acts 25:8. How could this be true if he had not kept the Sabbath?

53. The Sabbath is mentioned in the New Testament fifty-nine times, and always with respect, bearing the same title it had in the Old Testament, "the Sabbath day."

54. Not a word is said anywhere in the New Testament about the Sabbath's being abolished, done away with, changed, or anything of the kind.

55. God has never given permission to any man to work upon it. Reader, by what authority do you use - the seventh day for common labour?

56. No Christian of the New Testament, either before or after the resurrection, ever did ordinary work upon the seventh day. Find one case of that kind, and we will yield the question. Why should modem Christians do differently from New Testament Christians?

57. There is no record that God has ever removed His blessing or sanctification from the seventh day.

58. As the Sabbath was kept in Eden before the fall, so it will be observed eternally in the new earth after the restitution. (Isaiah 66:22-23.)

59. The seventh-day Sabbath was an important part of the law of God, as it came from His own mouth, and was written by His own finger upon stone at Sinai. (See Exodus 20.) When Jesus began His work, He expressly declared that He had not come to destroy the law. *"Think not that I am come to destroy the law, or the prophets."* Matthew 5:17

60. Jesus severely condemned the Pharisees as hypocrites for pretending to love God, while at the same time they made void one of the Ten Commandments by their tradition. The keeping of Sunday is only a tradition of men.

## 40 Bible Facts Concerning the First Day of the Week

1. The very first thing recorded in the Bible is work done on Sunday, the first day of the week. (Genesis 1: 1-5.) The Creator Himself did this. If God made the earth on Sunday, can it be wicked for us to work on Sunday?
2. God commands men to work upon the first day of the week. (Exodus 20.8-11.) Is it wrong to obey God?
3. None of the patriarchs ever kept it.
4. None of the holy prophets ever kept it.
5. By the express command of God, His holy people used the first day of the week as a common working day for 4,000 years, at least.
6. God Himself calls it a "working" day. (Ezekiel 46:1.)
7. God did not rest upon it.
8. He never blessed it.
9. Christ did not rest upon it.
10. Jesus was a carpenter (Mark 6:3) and worked at His trade until He was thirty years old. He kept

the Sabbath and worked six days in the week, as all admit. Hence, He did many a hard day's work on Sunday.

11. The apostles worked upon it during the same time.

12. The apostles never rested upon it.

13. Christ never blessed it.

14. It has never been blessed by any divine authority.

15. It has never been sanctified.

16. No law was ever given to enforce the keeping of it. Hence it is no transgression to work upon it. "Where no law is, there is no transgression." Romans 4:15 (See also 1 John 3:4.)

17. The New Testament nowhere forbids work to be done on it.

18. No penalty is provided for its violation.

19. No blessing is promised for its observance.

20. No regulation is given as to how it ought to be observed. Would this be so if the Lord wished us to keep it?

21. It is never called the Christian Sabbath.

22. It is never called the Sabbath day at all.

23. It is never called the Lord's day.

24. It is never called even a rest day.

25. No sacred title whatever is applied to it. Then why should we call it holy?

26. It is simply called the "first day of the week."

27. Jesus never mentioned it in any way, never took its name upon His lips, so far as the record shows.

28. The word Sunday never occurs in the Bible at all.

29. Neither God, Christ, nor inspired men ever said one word in favour of Sunday as a holy day.

30. The first day of the week is mentioned only eight times in all the New Testament. (Matthew 28:1; Mark 16:2, 9; Luke 24:1;
John 20:1, 19; Acts 20:7; 1 Corinthians 16:2)

31. Six of these texts refer to the same first day of the week.

32. Paul directed the saints to look over their secular affairs on that day. (1 Corinthians 16:2)

33. In all the New Testament we have a record of only one religious meeting held upon that day, and even this was a night meeting. (Acts 20:5-12)

34. There is no intimation that they ever held a meeting upon it before or after that.

35. It was not their custom to meet on that day.

36. There was no requirement to break bread on that day.

37. We have an account of only one instance in which it was done. (Acts 20:7)

38. That was done in the night - after midnight. (Verses 7-11) Jesus celebrated it on Thursday evening (Luke 22), and the disciples sometimes did it every day (Acts 2:42-46)

39. The Bible nowhere says that the first day of the week commemorates the resurrection of Christ. This is a tradition of men, which contradicts the law of God. (Matthew 15:1-9) Baptism commemorates the burial and resurrection of Jesus. (Romans 6:3-5)

40. Finally, the New Testament is totally silent with regard to any change of the Sabbath day or any sacredness for the first day.

Here are one hundred plain Bible facts upon this question, showing conclusively that the seventh day is the Sabbath of the Lord in both the Old and New Testament.*

*Reprinted from a tract published by the Review and Herald Publishing Association about the year 1885.

This material was printed from *100 Amazing Facts About The Sabbath And Sunday* | Sabbath Truth.   Retrieved from

https://www.sabbathtruth.com/free-resources/article-library/id/928/100-amazing-